Cash Confident

PRAISE FOR *CASH CONFIDENT*

"Brie's words inspire action while oozing heart… this funny guide will help self-aware women break the scarcity cycle of 'Busy, broke, and exhausted' so they can laugh all the way to the bank."

—**GEORGE BRYANT**, *New York Times* Best-selling Author, host of *Mind of George Podcast*, and CEO of mindofgeorge.com

"Brie Sodano penetrates far beneath the surface of personal finance platitudes and shines light on the dark corners of our minds and habits that keep us from building wealth the way we want. With gripping stories and no-nonsense truth gained from her years of experience, she shows us the way to real sanity and riches. Don't flounder on the shipwreck of your own fuzzy thinking. Buy *Cash Confident* and eat it up right now so you can thrive."

—**CAROLYN LOVEWELL** (formerly Elliott), author of *Existential Kink*

"Brie Sodano's *Cash Confident: Practical Money Management for the Modern Woman* is a refreshing deep dive into the often-overwhelming world of personal finance. Brie's book stands out with its insightful approach to breaking free from the 'Busy, Broke, and Exhausted' cycle, a concept that resonates strongly with anyone looking to declutter their financial life. Brie's honest and practical advice empowers readers to take control of their finances in an achievable way. *Cash Confident* is a vital resource for those seeking to navigate their financial journey with clarity and confidence."

—**KATY WELLS**, host of *The Maximized Minimalist* podcast

CASH CONFIDENT

PRACTICAL MONEY MANAGEMENT FOR THE MODERN WOMAN

BRIE SODANO

NEW YORK
LONDON • NASHVILLE • MELBOURNE • VANCOUVER

CASH CONFIDENT
PRACTICAL MONEY MANAGEMENT FOR THE MODERN WOMAN

© 2025 Brie Sodano

All rights reserved. No portion of this book may be reproduced, stored in a retrieval system, or transmitted in any form or by any means—electronic, mechanical, photocopy, recording, scanning, or other—except for brief quotations in critical reviews or articles, without the prior written permission of the publisher.

Published in New York, New York, by Morgan James Publishing. Morgan James is a trademark of Morgan James, LLC. www.MorganJamesPublishing.com

Proudly distributed by Publishers Group West®

ISBN 9781636984667 paperback
ISBN 9781636984674 ebook
Library of Congress Control Number: 2024934134

Cover Design by:
Formatted Books

Interior Design by:
Chris Treccani
www.3dogcreative.net

Author Photo by:
Carrie Roseman
Carrie Roseman Studios

Morgan James BOGO™

A **FREE** ebook edition is available for you or a friend with the purchase of this print book.

CLEARLY SIGN YOUR NAME ABOVE

Instructions to claim your free ebook edition:
1. Visit MorganJamesBOGO.com
2. Sign your name CLEARLY in the space above
3. Complete the form and submit a photo of this entire page
4. You or your friend can download the ebook to your preferred device

Morgan James is a proud partner of Habitat for Humanity Peninsula and Greater Williamsburg. Partners in building since 2006.

Get involved today! Visit: www.morgan-james-publishing.com/giving-back

To Mike Sodano

CONTENTS

Acknowledgments   *xi*
Introduction   *xiii*

Chapter 1:	Why Budgets Fail	1
Chapter 2:	Breaking the Cycle of Busy, Broke, and Exhausted	15
Chapter 3:	The Truth Is in the Transactions	39
Chapter 4:	Free Up Cash Flow	51
Chapter 5:	Sophisticated Spending	81
Chapter 6:	Drop the Debt, Once and For All	93
Chapter 7:	The Invisible System	113
Chapter 8:	Stretching Your Financial Comfort Zone	133

Conclusion and Invitation   *149*
About the Author   *155*

ACKNOWLEDGMENTS

This book was a labor of love. I'd like to thank Nick Pavlidis for patiently helping me every step of the way, Elisa Palumbo for the endless feedback, and my clients for letting me see the inner workings of their hearts, minds, and money.

INTRODUCTION

I started my career in finance as an investment advisor in 2013. My meetings with clients often surprised me. People I would have guessed were massively successful with money were not. People I would have guessed had money struggles did not. In fact, everything I'd assumed about people and money was wrong.

Some of the assumptions I made include the following:

- Hard work equals good money.
- Good education equals high pay.
- A paycheck above six figures equals good savings habits.
- Lots of income equals feeling at peace with your money.
- People's fights about money were about money.

All of these assumptions were wrong. Everything I thought I knew about people and money was all assumptions. There was no real basis for any of these assumptions. I'd never had real conversations with people about money, so TV, news, and education were all I had to go on.

My clients were coming to see me with problems that better investment options could not solve. I started to look at my clients' cash flow to help make beautiful plans to pay off debt and start saving, but I found the plans were not being executed. At first, this baffled me because my clients were smart and successful and could follow a plan in other areas of their lives. What made money so much harder to deal with?

I started asking my clients deeper questions, questions that led us into the mind, heart, and soul of people and their ability to create their lives. The rabbit hole of the relationship with and use of money goes to the core of a person's ability to create their life. Problems with money were causing so much pain and suffering for people. Money or the lack thereof was driving decisions, and oftentimes clients were feeling powerless about their financial situations.

Once I understood that the plans and budgets were not working, I started to look at clients' habits, thought patterns, belief structures, judgments, stories, emotions, and in-the-body sensations. From there I could come up with solutions that better removed the obstacles between people and their dream lives.

The reason I wrote this book is to show you the deeper layers of how financial decisions are made so you can find plans and solutions that work. Many people waste decades of time trying plan after budget after spreadsheet in attempts to get their money right, but the practical solution doesn't address the root cause of the problem and the plan fails. The mainstream suggestions about money may work on paper, but they often don't work on the habit, mindset, or emotional levels, leaving people feeling like failures.

This book is the result of my working with thousands of people since 2013, and it outlines the process I use to work with clients. The purpose of this book is to give you practical money management systems and strategies that are based on the ways humans make decisions.

Most of my clients are people who earn between $50,000 and $500,000 per year, who had enough money to hire me. This book is for the ladies in the middle who are really doing it all. My hope is that this book will help you see how to use your money powerfully and to create the life you want.

Additional Resources

This book comes with a companion workbook, which can be downloaded for free at:
https://www.cashconfidentbook.com/workbook

CHAPTER 1:

Why Budgets Fail

Joann was completely desperate. She was working three different jobs, each of them a business she'd started out of fear that she didn't have enough. She felt like whenever she got a tiny bit ahead in one job, something broke in another. She was clocking in sixty-plus hours a week, all while trying to balance family life. What started out as passion projects quickly spiraled into weighty obligations. It didn't matter how much money she was making. She felt busy, broke, and exhausted all the time.

When Joann came to me as a client, she had substantial debt. She'd started a business as a solution to that debt, but as a result, she was busy, broke, and exhausted. She didn't even have time to cook dinner. She'd hit the takeout apps every night instead of cooking dinner, and when she did cook, she'd hit the grocery store multiple times per week to buy one meal at a time at the last minute.

As a result of all this money stress, her homelife was suffering. She felt pulled between her financial goals and her marriage, which created a lot of strain on her and her husband. She felt trapped in a never-ending cycle of overworking causing overspending and overspending requiring overworking.

She is smart, capable, and passionate about achieving her financial goals, but she was set up for failure from the beginning. She knew how to make great plans, but she was not executing the plan. At her best, she made some progress in the short term and then slid back whenever she got too busy or exhausted.

Why Joann Could Never Get Ahead

First, she convinced herself that money was scarce and that she needed multiple income streams to be doing well financially. This blinded her to the fact that one of the businesses—the least lucrative of the three—took up most of her energy and time and was really holding her back.

She wanted to build a real estate empire that would allow her to make money without having to work all day. But she was afraid to let go of one of her businesses because they each provided somewhat of a consistent income. She didn't see, however, that trying to run three businesses was actually the cause of her money problems, not the solution.

Second, she was putting so much of her free cash flow toward her debt that she remained in a state of scarcity. She never had enough money to pay for emergencies, so when things came up, she had to use credit again. She knew she needed savings for real estate, but again, everything went toward debt and left her with nothing available for real estate.

Moreover, everything she did was manual and convoluted. She had lots of bank accounts and even more credit cards, all with different rules and purposes. Her system made clarity of her financial situation basically impossible and caused her money management to be reactive. She had spreadsheets all over the place, which were all completed after the fact. Because she couldn't remember everything she and her husband were spending, she was budget blind at the cash register. She had no idea whether she could even afford what she was about to purchase. In fact, her husband was so nervous about her poor money habits that he hid money from her in case a big emergency happened so she wouldn't obsessively put it toward debt.

Furthermore, she also felt guilty taking money out of her business and charging for the full value of her services. This is something a lot of women entrepreneurs deal with on a daily basis.

How We Turned It Around

When I looked into her transactions, I saw a similar pattern that I see with a lot of people. She was spending way too much time and money on areas she didn't need to. For example, she would spend hours and hundreds of dollars shopping for the best organic foods but then wouldn't have the time and energy to cook.

Up until then, she had been trying to improve her life through buying some missing things, not with a holistic plan that actually had a chance of succeeding.

We immediately got started building her a better plan—one built on the truths of both money and human behavior. We talked deeply about her goals, helped her break bad habits, and replaced these bad habits with better ones.

By the end of the first year that we worked together, she had saved up more than $30,000, in addition to paying down debt and feeling like an absolute baddie. She finished her contract for one of her businesses and didn't renew it. She learned about a real estate niche she could get into easier. She set systems in place to support and automate most of what she needed to do. And she increased her income while decreasing her expenses.

Before we started working together, she was making $4,000 per month working sixty hours a week on three businesses. At the end, she was making $8,000 per month while working half that. All the while, she had set healthy boundaries in her life so that other people (ahem . . . family) didn't cause her to get off track.

Just a couple of years later, I talked with her again. She'd bought a piece of real estate that was making her thousands of dollars monthly, and she was about to close on a second property.

Even more important, Joann and her husband are so much happier. The financial fear and stress had been a major bone of contention. As the situation changed, their marriage improved and they're on the same page when it comes to their fabulous finances . . . and it's only getting better.

Believe it or not, Joann's story is common. After working with many smart and amazing women struggling with money over the years, I know that most financial plans fail for the same reasons. Most of the conventional money wisdom is cookie-cutter, extreme, and only good on paper.

The vast majority of financial plans are doomed to fail because they are made for the money and not the human being executing the plan. Trying to implement a plan that is energetically and psychologically incongruent with the way humans make decisions doesn't work, but when it's the only way you know, it is easy to blame yourself or make up stories about how bad with money you are.

The truth is you don't need to be a real estate mogul, Instagram influencer, or hotel heiress to build wealth. You just need a plan that works, for you dear human being reading this book. By understanding these seven money problems, you'll be equipped to create a plan that's designed to succeed.

1. Scarcity and the Busy, Broke, Exhausted Cycle

Scarcity is a trickster vibe that screws with your reality and decision-making. Scarcity creates a cycle that starts when someone feels there's not enough time, money, or energy in their life and ends by creating more scarcity. Scarcity starts as a thought or circumstance, quickly becomes a feeling, then reduces your mental functions and creates scarcity behaviors that spread scarcity throughout your life like a toddler with a handful of Nutella.

Think of the feeling of not having enough money to pay all your bills or getting a surprise bill. Really, close your eyes for a moment and go down that rabbit hole to notice how those thoughts very quickly change your state. Many women describe feeling a tightness as they get into scarcity, and that constricted feeling is your brain and body communicating about how you will probably die. Sound dramatic? It is, but let me explain.

Your brain is in charge of keeping you alive and lack of resources is a problem that obviously requires attention and action, so your brain sends a signal to your body. Your body receives the signal from your brain as a threat of starvation. So in reality, you may have a situation where you pay a late fee or go a week without spending cash, but your body is freaking out like you must hunt a wild beast for dinner or die alone in the woods with no Wi-Fi.

Once this happens, all bets are off. Your brain turns off most executive functioning to free up energy for your hunting expedition. Everything feels urgent and decision-making gets really weird. Focus narrows and tunnel vision sets in. As all the extra energy shows up in your body to take action, your brain function lowers. This is a recipe for creating more scarcity through weird decision-making and action-taking.

It's nearly impossible to make good financial decisions here.

If you make decisions and take action from a place of scarcity, you'll end up creating more scarcity. Time, money, and energy are all connected, and living in a state of scarcity looks like being busy, broke, and exhausted. That's why you have to address your scarcity mindset first and learn how to navigate the emotional and physical feelings of scarcity in the body. A moment in scarcity can derail even great financial plans and months of hard work. Before you pick up the balance sheet or credit card, go deep and analyze how scarcity affects you. You'll find out more than you think.

2. Blank Sheet Budgets Don't Work

Joann used another financial program that had her put together a "blank sheet" budget that allocated most of her money toward debt, encouraging her to eat bologna sandwiches until she was debt-free. However, she soon realized that her consistent focus on debt only made her debt *grow*. Why? Because the plans were only for her money. They didn't address what habits would need to change or what time and energy resources would be required to make that plan work. All her money would go toward debt, but then she'd be using the credit cards to cover takeout when she was too tired to cook, a longstanding habit.

A lot of people who try to get their financial situation under control will look at their expenses and income and write on a blank sheet budget where they want it to go.

But here's the problem: They never fully know where that money's going and what actions, behaviors, and habits need to change to make that new plan work in the long term. That's a recipe for disaster and disappointment. Plus, it is easy to take on the inadequacies of the plan as a personal failing, adopting a story about how you are bad with money.

Before you go reallocating your money, first decide what you want your money to stop doing—and what needs to change in your life to support that habit change. This is a place where you really need to look at your time and energy to make these changes happen.

Joann wasn't buying takeout because she didn't know it ruined her budget. She knew how to cook and had the ingredients. What she didn't have was energy at the end of the day, and that energy doesn't just magically show up because you made a new budget. She needed support and lifestyle changes to free up that energy and time if her plan was going to work.

3. We Overestimate the Value of Knowledge

If I had a dollar for every time someone came to me for a better budget or plan to pay off their debt, I'd be drinking Coronas on a hammock to the tune of "Margaritaville." When it comes to money, knowing what to do is only a small percentage of the decision-making. Almost all of the time, the real problem is not doing the things we know how to do.

When it comes to changing their financial life, people waste years, sometimes decades, changing plans and acquiring more knowledge when the real problem is lack of implementation of the plan.

The truth of building wealth and being financially successful is not just knowing what to do; it's knowing yourself and implementing a plan that works with you, not against you.

This means looking at the truth of your desires, habits, mindset, and feelings about money, then addressing any problems that come up. Joann had a ton of scarcity in her mindset, habits, and emotions. This scarcity would derail even the best of plans and make all of her knowledge useless.

4. Financial Habits Take Longer to Build

When you take the same action over and over again, your sweet brain turns it into a shortcut called a habit. Something will happen that triggers the habit, which causes a routine and ultimately looks for a reward for doing the habit.

Financial habits are harder to build than habits in other areas of life because you may not have to take an action with enough frequency for your brain to need to build a shortcut. The thing about habits is that your subconscious handles the action without input from the conscious mind. It runs on autopilot. The conscious brain can get in the way of building habits with money because it is always considering all the things you could be doing instead.

Let's say you want to save money from every paycheck and you get paid every other week. You can only take that action once in fourteen days. Saving money habitually usually requires some support from technology.

When I was an investment advisor, two clients signed up for 529 plans for their kids on the same day. One was a hairdresser. She made $40,000 per year and set up a plan for each of her kids for $50 per month on automatic deposit. The other was making $160,000 per year as a car salesperson, but she didn't want the automatic withdrawal from her paychecks, so she decided to send a check every month. At the end of the year, the hairdresser had $600 in each of her kids' college savings while the other only wrote two checks. There are a zillion reasons not to save, and when you have to think about it before you take the action, it is far less likely to happen. Using technological support for savings is the way to "cheat" your way to more financial success.

Many people try to build these habits without support or think habits are built over time, which generally leads to failure. Use technology to build out systems that help you manage your money, rather than counting on your already taxed conscious brain to make the decisions.

5. A Lack of Clarity or Courage to Face Desires

Money is a tool for creation—a tool to define what's important to us and what's not. Every time we do one thing with our money, we are not doing something else. So when we don't have clarity about what we want to do or don't have the courage to do what we *really* want, we end up wanting every useful thing we see an Instagram ad for. As a result, our money goes toward what's convenient or shiny, not what we truly care about.

I had a client who was really struggling to save for a vacation. She was saving to go to a little lake cottage two towns over. But when I talked with her, the face she made didn't seem to indicate she really wanted to do it. So I asked, "Do you really want to go on this vacation?" Turns out, she didn't. She saw the vacation as a family obligation, but she was still ready to spend her hard-earned money on something she didn't really care about.

The internal conflict about the vacation is why she had a tough time saving for it. She didn't want it badly enough to give up buying clothes or eating out, so it never happened.

I asked her to describe the vacation she *really* wanted to go on. She wanted to go to Napa Valley to visit the vineyards, taste all the wines, and stay in a fancy hotel with room service and spa services. Since she couldn't manage to save the money for the cheap trip to the lake cottage with the in-laws, she thought Napa was out of the question. She really wanted that new trip, so I helped her lay out a plan to save for what she really wanted.

Guess what? She did a much better job saving up for that vacation because she actually wanted it. She was willing to pack a salad for lunch and forgo trips to Macy's in order to go to Napa. She could look forward to it, and the trip was worth the trade-offs in her mind. She had an easier time getting to Napa than she did two towns over.

6. Changing Your Mindset Is Absolutely Necessary

When it comes to creating a life you love, your mindset dictates what you believe is possible and your actions will fit inside that possibility. If we have financial goals that we don't believe are possible, we will get in our own way.

Your mindset needs to grow to the size and shape of the life you want to live.

Learning how to observe your mind, break a belief, and install a new belief is critical to creating a successful plan. Your mindset needs to grow to the life you want to live. If you adopt the mindset of your end goal, you'll have it before you know it.

The important thing to remember about your mind is that it learned everything it knows from the past. If you use those past truths to determine your thought patterns and actions, you will recreate the past in the future. If you want a future that is drastically different from your past, then you have to change your thinking and actions. Often this requires you to take actions where you don't have evidence of past successes. It can be scary or even feel a little delusional to change your thinking drastically, but that is a requirement of changing your finances—and life—in a big way.

7. A Plan Is Not a System

A lot of people put plans together, but they don't put a system together to execute them.

When it comes to money, people's plans frequently never get paired with a system, making them expensive in terms of time and mental energy. Plans that require a lot of manual tracking, upkeep, and updating are way less likely to be successful. Building out a money management system, like you will learn in this book, will help you to stick to your plan and see the financial progress you want.

CHAPTER 2:

Breaking the Cycle of Busy, Broke, and Exhausted

Jess hired me because scarcity had a grip on her life that was making her sick. She was riddled with anxiety, and the stress of her life was carving wrinkles into her sweet face. She was deep in the cycle of busy, broke, and exhausted. She was working full-time as a high-level executive assistant. She had two small kids and a spouse who was less than helpful at home. She was also volunteering at the kids' after-school activities.

Money was a major source of stress, and she was constantly shopping for all the bargains in an attempt to stretch a buck. Her energy was depleted, and she often resented her spouse and kids because she was cleaning up after them, never getting a chance to replenish herself from exhaustion.

When we started working together, I could see that some of her money problems were caused by scarcity in her time and energy and that common money solutions would fall short because she did not have an extra minute or thought to spend.

The first step in getting your financial life growing, thriving, and blossoming is not a practical step. It is emotional and energetic. In this chapter, we will explore the mental, physical, and emotional state of scarcity. The reason we do this before we start making money moves is because you will encounter scarcity as you work your plan, and being able to manage yourself through scarcity will help you stay on track and be kind to yourself.

Breaking a scarcity cycle is one of the most underrated financial skills required for making progress and building wealth.

Three Primary Resources: Time, Money, Energy

In life, we have three primary resources. Think of them like primary colors. We can take these three resources of time, money, and energy and turn them into anything from a college degree to a thriving business or even a drug ring. Time, money, and energy are very closely related and fluid; they flow into each other. You go to work and turn your time and energy into money. When you buy takeout dinner, you turn your money back into time and energy by not having to take your time and energy to cook.

There is a cycle of Busy, Broke, and Exhausted that is heartbreakingly pervasive in the world today. The cycle happens when scarcity gets into your primary resources and spreads quickly. Let's imagine you wake up late for work today, creating a shortage of time, and you run out of the house and really feel the stress of being late for work. That stress is your energy being expended quickly, and by the time you get to work, you feel ready for a nap, or possibly a cocktail to unwind. Then a few hours go by and you are hungry, so you head out to turn your time, money, and energy into a deli sandwich.

Jess was using money to plug holes in her time or energy and vice versa. For example, she was spending hours each week grocery shopping to buy the cheapest granola, but the misuse of time left her scrambling all week. This is important to understand because if you have a time or energy problem that money is fixing with a Band-Aid, you will need to address that time or energy problem before the money solution will stick. The flip side is also true: If your time and energy are required to fix a money problem, you have to be sure you have those resources available regularly for that financial plan to work. For Jess, we had to work on getting her time and energy under control before anything with the money would stick.

What Is Scarcity?

Scarcity is complex because it is a mindset, an emotional state, and a physical state that creates cycles of action that create more scarcity. We live in a culture of scarcity, where people often wear their busyness as a weird badge of honor and work themselves to burnout while being in debt.

Scarcity usually starts in the mind because your brain is in charge of keeping you alive. It's always analyzing whether something is a threat to us. Our brains have not changed much in the last ten thousand years, and scarcity triggers a primitive survival adaptation. A lack of resources is considered dangerous to your brain and something that must be addressed immediately. This sends a signal to your body that something is threatening your safety, and your body freaks out because it picks up that message of scarcity like the threat of starvation—even if the thought was about running out of half-and-half for your morning coffee. Your body gets itself ready to go hunt for dinner so you don't die. This is all a little dramatic, but real nonetheless.

Your body moves into heroic action to save itself from this perceived shortage of food. The brain turns off its executive functioning area to conserve energy for your hunt. Focus narrows, so the only thing you can focus on is addressing the shortfall. A massive flood of energy flows through your body ready to take immediate action. Since your lack of resources will likely not be solved by hunting down a wild beast for supper, the whole experience can feel stressful, and the decisions we make in scarcity will generally create more scarcity.

Here is an example of a perfect storm of scarcity: Maggie's car was having trouble, so she dropped it off with the mechanic and called out of work. When she picked the car up, she found out it would require a few thousand dollars worth of repairs. This news triggered an acute scarcity response because she didn't have the money or credit available to fix the car. It also created a sense of urgency since she needed the car to get to work, and she'd already taken a day off. It was at this moment she decided to buy a new car rather than fix the car she had, a decision that would cost more than $40K because she didn't have access to $3K. She took Friday off work set on buying a new car. She went to several dealerships and couldn't find anything she wanted that was available immediately and in her price range. By Sunday, she felt desperate and ended up buying an SUV on a six-year loan at $600 per month. She was well above her budget.

This woman is smart, and when she looks back on the whole thing, she can see options and opportunities that did not occur to her while she was in scarcity. This is not because she is foolish or makes bad decisions, but because her executive function center was offline. We can see that scarcity disrupted her thinking, so she rushed to solve her immediate problem, even though it created more scarcity in her already stretched financial situation. This moment would stay with her for six years, the length of the car loan. This is an example of how actions taken in scarcity create more scarcity.

What is described above is acute scarcity. Mid- or low-grade scarcity can also have big impacts. Sometimes it isn't always immediate or it might not trigger a full survival response, but it is just as taxing on your mental capacity and decision-making faculties.

Mid- or Low-Grade Scarcity

Scarcity doesn't always trigger a full-on panic or hunting expedition. Sometimes it's more subtle. Scarcity can cause your brain to constantly problem solve in the background of your mind. This can cause mental exhaustion and anxiety. This kind of scarcity is so taxing on your brain that it is proven to lower IQ by twelve to fifteen points and cause impulsiveness in decision-making.[1] Sometimes scarcity even shows up in quirky ways that are personal to

---

[1] Anandi Mani et al., "Poverty Impedes Cognitive Function," *Science* 341, no. 6149 (August 29, 2013): 976–80, https://doi.org/10.1126/science.1238041.

you. When I experience mid-grade scarcity, I get annoyed with my husband for no real reason.

Scarcity is a survival mechanism, and experiencing scarcity is an indication that your brain still functions on primal instinct. Scarcity is not a thing you can just get rid of, nor would you want to. Sometimes clients will beat themselves up for falling back into scarcity, and that is unhelpful and unkind to themselves. Scarcity in time, money, or energy is a thing you will certainly experience and that doesn't mean anything is wrong.

In this chapter, we will discuss ways to navigate scarcity and move yourself through it. It is possible to move your mental and physical state from scarcity to abundance with some awareness and practice. You can even harness the focused attention and intense motivation scarcity has to offer you.

Scarcity Jam Hands

When my son was little, he was perpetually sticky. I joked about this and called the phenomenon "jam hands." Whenever he ate and touched anything, he would get sticky little handprints on everything. This kid could make a massive mess in just moments, and I share this with you because scarcity has jam hands too.

This is how scarcity operates: As soon as it gets into one of your three primary resources, it spreads like the stickiness of a small child with a jelly sandwich and gets absolutely everywhere. If you operate from a place of scarcity and try to act on your finances, you'll get that stickiness in places you didn't think was possible. It's a self-perpetuating cycle.

How to Know Whether You have Scarcity Jam Hands

If you're not sure whether scarcity has been calling the shots, I've broken down different ways that scarcity shows up in our body, mind, and behavior. The sooner you identify the signs, the sooner you'll understand how to fight it. Scarcity shows up in three separate places in our lives: our mind, body, and actions. It will serve you to become aware of what scarcity looks and feels like for you at both acute and low-grade levels. This kind of awareness will give you the opportunity to navigate through the scarcity before you take the action that creates more scarcity.

Scarcity in the Mind

Scarcity generally starts in the mind because your brain scans the world for danger and lack of resources is a pretty big deal. For lots of my clients, there is a scarcity rabbit hole of thought that leads surely and swiftly to scarcity in the body. Everyone's rabbit hole of mental scarcity is different, but here is an example.

> *I am pouring a cup of coffee and notice I am almost out of half-and-half. I think about going to the store for more, then the thought becomes a whole week of grocery shopping. The thought of how expensive groceries have gotten creeps into my mind. Then I remember my electricity and insurance and taxes have gone up too. I think, how am I going to make it when the whole world demands so much from me? Then I think I probably need to give my team a raise because their prices have gone up too.*

In a matter of moments, my mind drags me into the vibe of scarcity to the point where my body starts to feel it. Thinking a thought or two of scarcity isn't necessarily a problem, but when you think so many thoughts that you can feel your heart race, chest tighten, stomach clench, or any form of tightness, you have changed your emotional state or vibe.

The change in physical and emotional state is really important because that becomes the place that actions are taken from. Actions taken from scarcity create more scarcity and that is why I call it jam hands.

Action Step: Notice your scarcity triggers and your own rabbit hole of personal thoughts. Write these things down so you can be aware of when you are going down that rabbit hole.

Scarcity in the Body

Scarcity in the body is twofold. There is physical scarcity and emotional scarcity. Both emotional and physical scarcity will drive decision-making and actions.

Emotional scarcity may be described as feelings of inadequacy, being undeserving, unworthiness, or any flavor of not being enough. You can feel the emotional scarcity, but it is different from physical scarcity.

Physical scarcity is when your mind has freaked your body out to the point where it gets ready to go hunt down a wild beast in the forest. This response means your brain shuts down your executive functions while energy is being redirected to the body.

Scarcity in Action

Scarcity has a direct effect on our decisions, actions, habits, and behavior. It influences how we show up in the world, to our family, and with our finances. Oftentimes, scarcity makes our behavior more reactive, impulsive, and shortsighted. To stop this, we need to understand how scarcity shows up in our behavior.

Based on my client work and my own life, here are seven ways I've observed scarcity show up again and again:

1. Getting Rid of Money

When you have a story of "there's never enough money," having money can be deeply uncomfortable, especially if you don't trust yourself to make great choices with it. Often, clients feel like they waste money, so when they have more than they are used to, they want to quickly "do something good with the money, before I do something stupid with it." This generally causes hasty decision-making that comes from a place of fear, mistrust, and discomfort.

2. Withholding Money

On the flip side of the coin, many people fear a low bank account. So, in an act of financial self-preservation, they hold on to money when it's due to go out. This often means paying bills late, skipping fun life events, delaying home repairs, and being stingy with loved ones. Scarcity convinces the person that they "should" hold on to the money. This causes money to be spent on late fees, problems that grow into bigger expenses, and money to stop flowing through life energetically.

3. Overgiving

Scarcity can cause overgiving, a situation where giving feels like an obligation or something other than generosity. This may look like agreeing to bake for the PTA bake sale when you are already stretched for time or energy and resenting the whole thing. It may look like compulsively picking up the tab for a friend's lunch, even when it doesn't fit in your budget. It may look like taking responsibility for others' emotions. It may look like working outside of your agreements with an employer or your clients and not being paid for the extra mile.

4. Undercharging

Scarcity may show up as a fear of not having work or jobs. This usually feels like a "I gotta take what I can get" kinda vibe, which generally lends itself to being underpaid, scope creep in the gig economy, or unpaid hours on salary. The fear of not having enough creates the circumstances where you don't have enough. Once I had a client who was charging her biggest client $1,000 per month for design work that was worth $4,000 per month. She was so afraid to lose the $1,000 of steady income that she lost $3,000 of potential payment for months until we worked through it.

5. Misuse of Time and Energy

When scarcity is in your money and your brain is on power-saver mode, you may find yourself using a tremendous amount of time or energy to save a buck. This moves the financial scarcity back into time and energy and perpetuates more scarcity.

One of my clients had a kid who was obsessed with cucumbers and ate a ton. She found that the cucumbers were $10 less at Costco than at the grocery store. As a result, she would go to Costco every week. This cost her a thirty-minute drive, there and back, gas in the car, and often a $12 impulse purchase. Her effort to save $10 was outweighed by the cost of the energy to go shopping twice, the hour in the car, the gas to get there, and the impulse purchase.

6. Complicating Things

Scarcity raises the question, what can I do? When we are all jazzed up on adrenaline but don't have an actual solution, many times we will just add complications to our systems or financial situation. The complications create more scarcity in the future by taking away the ability to clearly see and understand what is actually going on with the money.

Once I met with a client who had seven bank accounts and twelve credit cards. Some of the bank accounts only paid one bill and some of the credit cards were used to transfer balances. The system she had was so convoluted she couldn't get a clear picture of what was going on. We tried. I asked her to draw a picture and neither of us could follow it. This created more scarcity because she didn't know when she was out of money. The credit allowed her to spend beyond her means, and the complications stopped her from being able to see she was overextended.

7. Avoidance and Ambivalence

Scarcity can trigger a freeze response too. This may look like not opening statements to avoid checking the balances on your bank account or credit card. You may put off opening a 401(k) for a long time or avoid other financial actions. When scarcity is so entwined in the fabric of your life, you may feel ambivalent, like an effort to make a change won't make a difference, so YOLO.

How to Navigate Scarcity

Scarcity can feel scary in the moment, but it is something that you can navigate through. In time, the focus and high level of energy that come with scarcity can even be harnessed. That requires a lot of self-awareness. These skills are so important to learn because scarcity is not something you can just get rid of. Scarcity shows up to protect you, motivate you, and move you into action.

Cultivate Awareness

First, we want to notice and track our scarcity triggers. What are the circumstances, thoughts, actions, and situations that bring up scarcity in us?

Second, observe the mental rabbit hole. Notice all your regular fears or thoughts that lead to the sinking feeling of scarcity in the body.

Third, notice what scarcity feels like in your body. Where are the sensations? Describe them in detail. Notice any desire to move. Think about moments of intense scarcity and moments of mid- or low-grade scarcity, as the sensations will probably be different.

Fourth, notice any actions that you took from scarcity. Become aware of any regular actions that happen often. Think back to a moment of acute scarcity and then to moments of moderate scarcity. Remember, you may take actions not on the list of common scarcity actions we just went through.

The full awareness of what scarcity looks like in circumstances, sounds like in the mind, and feels like in the body or emotions is the starting point.

Rewire the Brain and Body for Abundance

Scarcity and abundance are both available all the time. What we see is a perception issue. You can train your brain to experience more abundance. This is an activity that helps to rewire the synapses in the brain. It must be done regularly for an extended period of time to make a difference.

There are three different vibes that help to create a sense of safety and abundance with money. The goal of these practices is to change your state. We will use the mind to bring focus to gratitude, appreciation, or plenty until we feel that matching feeling in our body. The shift in the feeling of your vibe, mood, or body is the magic sauce.

Gratitude Is the Vibration of Having
Most books on manifesting or the law of attraction suggest a daily gratitude practice and I agree completely. Look around at your life to take a moment to be grateful for what you have. Practicing gratitude can be done in many ways. Again, the way to know that you are done is by feeling the shift in your state, essentially the warm and fuzzies. Here are some variations on cultivating gratitude.

Financial Gratitude
Make a list of all your money, assets, income sources, available credit, and tools to make money. Be with each item for a moment of gratitude.

Love Gratitude
Pick a human you love and write in depth the qualities and characteristics in them that you are grateful for.

Bounce-Back Gratitude

Write thank-you notes and mail them for any old thing. This is an especially powerful practice because it takes a thought of gratitude and then puts it into action. Often, it makes someone else's day, and that kind of gratitude bounces back to you. You can take the same idea and send text messages.

Present Moment Gratitude

Close your eyes for a moment and be grateful for the comfort you are experiencing right now. It could be something like your chair supporting your tush, the breeze, or the smell of dinner.

You can get creative with these practices. You can do micro practices throughout your day or write a long list. Again, the benefit comes from intentionally directing your thoughts to what you already have and then feeling the safe and abundant feeling in your body.

Appreciation Is the Vibration of Growing

What we appreciate grows, and appreciation is cultivated by acknowledging, speaking, and acting in kind.

You can start appreciating all the things money does for you, looking forward to all the new things it can be doing for you.

Appreciation also works great with spouses, lovers, coworkers, and children. People love to be appreciated, so the more you can give out, the more love and support come your way.

Pour Your Appreciation onto Everything You Want More Of

Plenty is the vibration of abundance.

Abundance is everywhere, all the time. When you focus on the plenty in your life, you tune yourself into the abundance.

Take a few moments each day to notice and appreciate the plenty in your life. The key here is to keep the time frame for your thoughts to today.

You can start in your house. *I have plenty of toothpaste, so much toothpaste I couldn't even use it all today. I have an abundance of toothpaste. I have plenty of clothes; I couldn't even wear them all today. I have an abundance of clothes. I have plenty of butter; I couldn't even use it all today. I have an abundance of butter.*

You can take the same idea and apply it to abundance of space, natural beauty, or anything else.

These practices are all helpful to train your brain to focus on growing what you have and are growing. These practices are less helpful in getting from acute scarcity to OK.

Navigating Intense Scarcity

The faster you can become aware of scarcity, the easier it is to address. If you have a few thoughts taking you down the rabbit hole, the situation is easier to come back from than if you think yourself into a panic. Feeling the intensity of scarcity is easier to address than once you take an action from scarcity that will most likely create more scarcity.

If you are mentally going down the rabbit hole of scarcity in your thoughts, you want to change the direction of them. For example, you can put on a song you love to sing to break the pattern. If that is not possible or your mind is tumultuous, you can just say "Thank you" out loud over and over again for a few moments.

The point here is to stop going down the mental rabbit hole.

If the scarcity is in the body, then you want to get your heart rate up for about two minutes. This is enough to close the fight-or-flight response loop and get your executive functioning back online.

If your intense scarcity feels like hitting a wall or intense avoidance, you can dance around, shaking your body vigorously. If your body asks to yell or make any movement, go with it. This can help to close open freeze responses.

Sit On Your Hands

If you are having thoughts or intense feelings of scarcity, do not take action. Sit with the feelings until they pass because taking action creates more scarcity. Give yourself time to let your brain and body come back to center before you make any moves.

Remember, when your focus is narrowed, you cannot see how many great options are truly available to you.

Breaking the Busy, Broke, and Exhausted Cycle

When I started working with Jess, I could see the scarcity was layers deeper than just the money. She didn't have time or energy to do most of the tasks I would assign her.

She cried in my office, feeling backed into a corner in every aspect of her life, feeling perpetually busy, broke, and exhausted. The first thing we did was order her a dumpster. We started with decluttering her house because she had two small kids and the mess was a major energy suck. She couldn't get a moment of peace because all their stuff was constantly yelling at her to be tidied up. Plus, her spouse didn't seem to notice the mess, and her resentment toward him was inching them ever closer to divorce. She and her family took a weekend to clear out their house—removing twenty cubic yards of crap and thirty-six bags of donations.

Clearing out the house freed up her energy. Instead of rage-cleaning, she could rest and recuperate. This helped her marriage a ton. The decluttering also changed what she would allow in her house while reducing her appetite for shopping. She stopped going to thrift stores because she liked the amount of stuff she had at home.

Then we went through her transactions looking for ways to free up time, money, and energy. One of the biggest places she was overspending in time, money, and energy was the grocery store. She was going to three or four stores a week bargain hunting the best deals. This was actually causing her to spend much more than clients with a similar family size. We cut her shopping to one store per week, and this saved her $75 per week, three to four hours of her time, and so much stress. From there, she had the time and energy to do what it took to increase her income and pay down her debts, all while saving more money for vacations and education funds for her kids.

It takes time and mental energy to change your relationship with money. This is especially true if you have any emotional resistance to money or tendencies to avoid money. When you can get time, money, and energy back from a single habit change, that is a great place to start because it breaks the cycle of being busy, broke, and exhausted.

Do the Work: Scarcity

As discussed in the chapter, there are seven ways I commonly see scarcity showing up for clients in their decisions, actions, habits, and behavior. In a journal or notebook, record how each behavior listed below shows up in your life. You can also find this activity in the companion workbook, which can be downloaded for free at https://www.cashconfidentbook.com/workbook.

1. Getting Rid of Money
   - Stocking up or hoarding goods.
   - Buying from a place of "I better get this now while I have the money."
   - "I don't know whether I have the cash or I need this now, but whatever, I'm buying it."
2. Withholding Money
   - Not paying bills on time.
   - Skipping basic maintenance or repairs.
   - Avoiding events and functions or appearing stingy.
3. Overgiving
   - Donating to causes when you don't have the cash.
   - Contributing more than you have to give.
   - Volunteering your time when you're already busy.
4. Undercharging
   - Thinking you have to take what you can get.

- Not charging enough for your time, effort, and skill set.
5. Misuse of Time or Energy
    - Going to multiple grocery stores to save a few dollars on food.
    - Driving two towns away to get cheaper gas.
6. Complicating Things
    - Opening more bank accounts than youBr need.
    - Overthinking purchases.
    - Adding rules to financial situations.
7. Avoidance and Ambivalence
    - Not opening bank accounts or credit card statements to avoid seeing the balance.
    - Avoiding taking important financial actions for fear of their outcome.

Scarcity in Your Body

Close your eyes and feel into scarcity for a moment. This exercise may bring up some unwanted feelings, but that's the point. Pay attention to how scarcity feels in your body. In your mind, bring attention to the feeling of scarcity in your body. Take a moment to pause and feel each of your body parts. Reflect on the physical sensations in your body (hot, heavy, tight, sharp, stabbing, etc.). Does the sensation have a color or texture associated with it? Record these feelings in your notebook or journal.

Rewire the Brain for Abundance through Gratitude

Complete this exercise immediately after completing the one above. We are going to feel into gratitude first. Open up to a blank page in your journal or notebook. Set a timer for three minutes. As soon as you hit start, begin writing down all the things you are grateful for. Don't stop writing until the timer goes off.

Finally, go to the next blank page in your journal or notebook and number the lines from one to ten. Take a moment to think about all the things that surround you each and every day. What ten things in life make you feel abundant?

CHAPTER 3:

The Truth Is in the Transactions

A lice hired me to find the money she thought she was missing. She and her husband made multi-six figures, but they were often running low. Alice had run the numbers thousands of times and had her hard expenses down, but she couldn't seem to find any discretionary money, even though it was there on paper.

When I first looked at her transactions, I noticed lots of small, recurring payments. Charity donations, news subscriptions, political group contributions, and in-app purchases, among other things. I asked her how much she was spending on subscriptions per month, and she said $150, but that wasn't true at all.

I decided that Alice's microtransactions needed their own category to help her understand how they were adding up. Once we separated the purchases from her other spending, she finally saw how the small habits turned into $800 a month.

Upon closer inspection, she realized that her spouse and children were spending in those little ways too. The whole family was making multiple microtransactions every single day.

This isn't just important for Alice. So many of my clients suffer from the same issue. And now that you understand why plans fail and the emotional side of money management, you're ready to dig into your own transactions too. That's what we'll do here.

The Truth Is in the Transactions

If you've ever opened up a bank or credit card statement and thought, "I've been robbed," and upon further inspection, you recall all of the transactions, this chapter is going to help you move beyond the mental limitations of accounting.

When it comes to finding the accuracy around your spending habits, the truth is in the transactions. I've asked thousands of people, "How much do you spend on groceries?" and every single time anyone has answered, they were wrong. This is because mental accounting is flawed. Our brains are not wired for accuracy in that way, so we do our best to remember, but it's not accurate.

When you want to use your money to create a difference in your life, the first thing to do is figure out where your money is going. That is what you will learn in this chapter.

Facing Procrastination or Avoidance

Looking at your transactions can bring up some feelings, maybe a lot of feelings. I've noticed this step of the financial journey can cause some avoidance or procrastination. If the idea of looking at your transactions makes you want to clean the entire house before you get started, that is normal and OK. The trick to moving through the avoidance is to acknowledge your feelings and give them some attention.

Connie told me she didn't have time to review her transactions, which was her assignment from our previous meeting. This happened right at the beginning of the pandemic, and I knew that she had literally been at home for the last fourteen days, so she had had time. I asked, "Why don't you want to do it?" and she told me, "I feel so ashamed. When I look at my money, I see every bad choice I ever made and can imagine my dad being disappointed with me."

Whoo . . . that's heavy and the exact reason she was avoiding her transactions. Once we acknowledge and feel the feelings, the resistance starts to lift. Be kind to yourself as you move through your emotions.

Acknowledging feelings is more important than you'd imagine when it comes to money. Here is how you do it. First, locate the sensation of the emotion. The sensation is in your body; it's not a story. You can say to yourself something to the effect of, "I feel a tightness in my chest." You can touch the area of your body where the sensation is or squeeze your muscles in that area to help build the connection between your mind and body. You can ask yourself what the sensation in your body represents to you. Meet the sensation with curiosity and kindness for yourself. Each emotion you have comes with information to help you.

When Connie acknowledged the shame she felt about her money and the perceived disappointment from her dad, that emotion was released and she was able to look at her transactions. Treating herself with kindness and curiosity helped her to build trust in herself in her relationship with money.

Tracking Your Money

Tracking your money is not the same thing as reading your statements. The goal of money tracking is to see the big picture, to understand what your money is funding and creating. The goal here is to see the habits and patterns. Now that you can manage your thoughts, feelings, and actions through scarcity, we can start to get into your money.

Tracking your transactions is the starting point because it provides you with clarity on exactly what is happening. This is important because when it comes to learning to spend your money intentionally to create the life you want, it often means stopping spending on things that don't create it. In this chapter, you will learn how to track your money and free up the time, money, and energy required to build the life you dream of.

Tracking your money doesn't have to be complicated or scary. I remember the days of writing down every purchase and manually adding them to a spreadsheet. As totally fun as that was, technology has made tracking your expenses easier than ever. I suggest using software to categorize your transactions—something that allows all of your accounts to be connected and aggregated. I prefer software that has charts and colors, as that helps with clarity. What I will teach you here applies to most of the software programs available.

Before Alice and I worked together, she was using a series of spreadsheets to track her money. She would manually import her transactions to the sheet, and then categorize from there. This was a solid amount of effort, but the method was so cumbersome that her effort wasn't effective. First, she hated doing it and that was its own problem. Second, it took a lot of time and effort, and third, the sheet couldn't exactly show trends or improvements.

She switched to user friendly software when we worked together so it could do the work of compiling all the data. As she started tracking, she was able to set rules for categorization that increased the speed and ease. She was able to see trends and improvements.

How to Track Your Money

Before you get started setting up an account with the money-tracking software of your choice, make a list of all your accounts with usernames and passwords. This will help you complete the task in one sitting and reduce frustration. Be sure to have your phone next to you, for any two-factor authentication. Open your software account and connect your financial accounts.

Look at the categories available in your chosen software platform. Generally, there are way more categories than you need. Check to see whether you can add a category or tags.

Think about what categories you want and need. You want the least number of categories possible to create maximum clarity. Using too many categories stops you from seeing the forest through the trees.

Put all of your regular bills under one category. There will probably be tons of options like housing, auto, insurance, etc. Find the category name that fits household bills best and use that.

Food tends to be an area that can be broken down further. Most money tracking software offers these categories: Groceries, Fast Food, Restaurants, Bars, Coffee Shops. I suggest using a minimum of two categories for food: Groceries and Restaurants. If food spending is a large part of your expenses, break it down a little further.

Shopping is a category that can be broken down into further categories. It is worth it to track household shopping, clothes, holidays, or gifts. You may want to add a tag for shopping that is one-time or seasonal. For example, if you go to Home Depot for the supplies to fix a staircase, that is one-time, versus going to Home Depot to buy chrysanthemums and fabulous fall decor, which is seasonal.

Credit cards work like bank accounts inside the software. You will see a charge as an expense when the money goes from you to a store. When you pay your credit card bill, it looks like a transfer. You transfer your money in your bank account to the negative balance of your credit card.

Most software programs will allow you to hide an account, too. This can be useful if your business account or kid's bank account is showing up in your software, which can happen when you are the signer.

When you start looking at your transactions, start by checking your income. Make sure all of your income is showing.

Organize Your Transactions

After working with so many clients over the years, I've developed a system of organization that'll help you make sense of where your money's going and why. It's popular to use what we call "line items," like medical bills, car repairs, and the mortgage. I disagree with this approach because it quickly creates too many categories to keep track of, which only creates needless stress.

Instead, my approach involves sorting your transactions by purpose. This means that things like bills—rent/mortgage, utilities, insurance, etc.—are all under one roof. Regular expenses are under one roof. Money for savings and retirement are under one roof. You get the picture.

Here are the five primary categories:

1. **Investments:** Investments, retirement, nest egg money. This is where all long-term wealth goes.
2. **Bills:** Think of all your monthly recurring payments like the mortgage or rent, utilities, or insurance. This is where your money goes first.

3. **Working Capital:** You know that car repair you know you need, but you're still surprised when your car breaks down? This account helps you prepare for that. That way, those "unexpected expenses" are already taken care of.
4. **Important Things:** If you've been itching to replace the kitchen cabinets or take that tropical cruise, this category is for those expenses. If it matters to you, save for it.
5. **Pocket Money:** Groceries, date night, and other "fun" expenses come from this account. This account should be depleted and restored every single month. Don't save any money here.

You can use additional categories to look at something, like Alice's microtransactions, more closely. Once Alice saw how much money her family was spending on tiny purchases, she was able to work with them to change that habit. Her family redirected that money and was able to visit family in Europe a year later.

Once you do the work of categorizing your transactions, you can start to use that information to see any place you feel your money is wasted, used inefficiently, or spent on things you don't truly want. In the next chapter, you will learn how to use the information from your tracked transactions to free up cash flow.

When it comes to tracking your money, look at the expectation of what is reasonable for a certain category and then look at the habits and totals rather than dollar amounts of individual transactions.

Do the Work: Use Software to Track Your Money

In the age of technology, there are dozens of apps that can help you track your money. Here's how to do the research to choose the app that will work best for you. The effort is worth it to understand what is happening in your transactions. You can also find this activity in the companion workbook, which can be downloaded for free at https://www.cashconfidentbook.com/workbook.

Here are the common things I look for when choosing a money tracking app:

1. Ease of use. You want something that looks like it will be easy for you to learn and use. If the screenshots of the app are already bulky and confusing looking, move on.
2. Authority. Look for an app developed by a company that is already trusted in the financial field. Check what security they offer and the relationships they have formed with other financial institutions.

3. Popularity. The more people use an app, the more it is supported. Look for one that is recommended by other companies with authority in the financial industry and the general public.
4. Ability to customize and organize categories. You need to have the ability to organize your spending into categories as I outlined in this chapter. Look for this feature to be listed under the functions of the app you intend to use.
5. Multiple ways to access the app. Mobile and desktop versions are available.

Still not sure what you should be looking for? Ask a friend or put the question out there on social media. I find people love to talk about the apps they use for money tracking. Whenever someone asks in the Cash Confident Community Facebook group, people answer.

CHAPTER 4:

Free Up Cash Flow

Eve came to see me as she was feeling tight and restricted with regard to her money. She had some debt that was eating up her free cash flow. She is a mom of two girls and has her own business. She took the steps to free up her cash flow, and within a few months, she had freed up $850 per month and redirected that to building a sweet deck around her pool. The other cool thing is she reduced the amount of time and mental energy she was spending shopping, and she redirected that time and energy to her business, which really grew in the following year.

Starting with one-time actions, she called her vendors for promo pricing and got her credit card interest reduced by 11 percent. This freed up her cash flow by $300 per month, and she redirected that $300 to an old loan that was close to being paid off. Next, she set up systems to be more efficient in the household procurement. This reduced the amount of time, energy, and money she was spending at the stores. This freed up another $200 per month, which she redirected to her loan. That old loan was paid off in no time, and then she increased her credit card payments.

She wasn't doing too much emotional spending, but looking at her emotions and money gave her clarity on what she wanted to prioritize: family togetherness. She noticed she would often spend time with her girls shopping, and she wanted more high-quality interactions. She didn't want her girls to equate shopping with love. She decided that she wanted to add a great big deck around her pool so she and her family would have plenty of space to be together.

It took about eight months to pay off her consumer debts, and when the debts were repaid, she had $850 per month to use toward the deck.

Once you have thoroughly tracked your transactions, we can really get in there to free up cash flow to redirect toward your dream life. This is both the juiciest and hardest part of money management. This is the place where actions change.

Clarity around desire and the life you are building is important at this stage because asking yourself to change a habit or give something up in exchange for something you don't really want doesn't work so well.

The process I use around this is threefold. We are looking to free up time, money, and energy all at once so that we can direct all those resources to building the dream life.

Identify the Waste

The first thing to look for in your transactions is anything you consider to be wasteful. It could be something like a magazine subscription you don't actually read, a gym membership you don't use, a pantry so full that a can of peaches from 2007 is way in the back, or clothes from two seasons ago with the tags still on.

What Is Waste?

Waste is something that
- Is unused or unwanted
- Could be lost or sacrificed and not missed
- Contributes nothing constructive to your life

Generally, financial waste is caused by overbuying or not wanting to let go. For example, many clients willingly pay for a gym membership they don't use because it feels like a loss to let it go. This can turn into a cycle, where we don't want to let go of something because we spent the money on it, but we didn't get the benefit.

Scan Your Transactions

While you are looking at your transactions for waste, think about your purchases and whether you used them. Make a list of anything you bought but didn't use. Take a look around your house to look for unopened boxes, old food, unworn clothes, etc. Note each store and item on this list. If you notice any patterns about time of day, day of the week, or emotional state while shopping, keep a note of that too.

One-Time Money-Saving Actions

When freeing up cash flow, I like to start with one-time actions because they generally don't require a habit change or big sacrifice. I will warn you; it can be a pain in the rump though and will probably take a little longer than you hope.

Shop Your Vendors

Look at your transactions and make a list of any product or service you may be able to switch out for one that is less expensive. For example, you may be able to shop for a better deal on your car or homeowners insurance policy, call your cell phone carrier to see whether they have any promotions, or call your credit card companies to ask them to lower your interest rates. This is a bit of a pain, but the one-time action often yields a good result.

Clear the Clutter

Wasteful spending can often be seen as clutter in the home. Clearing out the clutter in closets, pantries, and spare rooms is a big step in cultivating a more abundant life. When we have too much stuff, we expend a lot of time and energy to find, organize, and clean the stuff. For lots of women, clutter makes their home feel noisy—like all the stuff is asking to be picked up and put away and that steals peace and rejuvenation. Energetically clearing clutter creates space for new energy to come into the house. On a practical level, when you know what you've got and where it is, you are less likely to buy it again.

Jess was a client of mine who struggled with her money for years. She was always bargain hunting and buying things at thrift stores to get the best deal. At our meetings, she would cry in frustration about her money and about her husband not helping with the home or kids. She was even angry and resentful with her small children because she was always picking up after them. We ordered a dumpster, and she cleared out twenty cubic yards of stuff, while donating thirty-six big black trash bags. I wish I had taken a before and after picture of the change in her after getting rid of her clutter. No lie, her curls were bouncier, her face looked younger, and her money situation improved drastically because she stopped all unnecessary shopping.

Adjust Your Tax Withholdings
I had a client whose cash flow was so tight that she was pinching actual pennies every week, but then she got a $12K tax refund. She would use that refund to pay off credit card debt she'd incurred throughout the year. While a little tax refund is a nice surprise, letting the government borrow your money with no interest for a year isn't the best financial move. Especially, if you are using credit to make ends meet. You can adjust your withholdings on your W-4 form. Talk to your accountant to choose the withholding amount that is best for you.

Take Action
Take your lists of what actions to take, what calls to make, and what subscriptions to cancel, and start doing the things. Keep track of how much money you free up. Celebrate your no sacrifice shifts. Then apply that cash flow to something you want. Your cash flow will feel the same, but you will be making progress toward your desires.

Redirect That Cash Flow Right Away

When you start freeing up the cash flow, redirect it right away. If you want to increase your debt payments or investments, keep track of your free cash flow and start sending those bigger checks right away. Your cash flow will feel the same, but if you let the money flow into your regular spending accounts, it will likely disappear.

Increase Efficiency

After you go through your transactions to find and redirect wasted resources, then you can start increasing household efficiency. This part is straight freakin' magic. The suggestions and methods I teach here are tested and they work, especially for busy ladies. Efficiency is super important because this is where you free up the time, energy, and money to create life the way you want it.

Jen was the epitome of busy, broke, and exhausted. She is a fortysomething executive with a toddler. She was exhausted because she never had time to rest, and she never had time to rest because she was running out to the store five to twelve times a week. She wasn't thinking ahead, and her inefficiency was costing hundreds of dollars, taking hours of her time, and causing her stress every single week.

The Big Cost of Shopping Small

Shopping is more than making a list or thinking, "We need more eggs . . ." When working with clients, I make it clear that setting up systems helps to avoid the busy, broke, and exhausted cycle. Why? Because stores are designed to get the maximum cart value and keep you coming back for more. Every time you shop, you expose yourself to quite a bit of psychological manipulation designed to get deep into your purse.

Break the Habit of Shopping Small

Imagine a coworker brings a box of donuts to work. How many donuts will you eat? One, maybe two. A donut registers as a whole treat and triggers a certain amount of consideration before eating and satisfaction during or after eating it. Now, imagine a coworker brings in a box of Munchkins donut holes. How many will you eat? One every time you walk by. The same thing happens with shopping.

More Shopping = More Spending

Retailers have spent billions of dollars and decades researching how to get the maximum cart value. Every item on the shelf, the music, the store layout, the smell of Starbucks fresh brewing coffee in the front of the store is all on purpose. The more you shop, the more stores you are in, and the more you expose yourself to increased want and impulse purchases.

Shopping in all forms is a big part of the household responsibilities, which can be a huge drain on time and energy resources. Making your household procurement efficient helps to free up time, money, and energy for better things.

Small Transactions & Habit Blindness

One time, a client was in my office who was really benefiting from our work, but she also was asking to break her contract and quit her program before she was finished. She didn't think she had the money, and her tight cash flow was causing stress. We reviewed her transactions and found she was spending about $600 per month on home decor and snacks. What I realized in that meeting was that she was spending unconsciously. She was on autopilot and wasn't considering the cost of her purchases if they were below $42.

As we went through her transactions, I kept asking her one question: What did you buy? Anything more than $42 she could remember and tell me what she bought. Anything less became vague. What I realized was purchases made on autopilot are hard to address because we don't remember them as clearly, and they don't seem like a problem because they are small spends.

Review Your Own Transactions

We each have different thresholds for when spending goes from something small to something that requires consideration. The number may be different for different aspects of spending. For example, my autopilot number for food spending is higher than for clothes. Everyone has their own mental framework.

When you review your transactions, try to remember what you bought. If the memory is clear, you probably made that spending decision consciously. If the memory is vague, you were probably spending on autopilot. You can also ask yourself how much you just spent as you are walking out of a store. If you can't remember as you walk to the car, that purchase didn't get a lot of conscious consideration.

Our subconscious brain is running the show of our lives most of the time. This helps to conserve energy for conscious thinking, which is expensive to your brain and body in terms of calorie consumption. Decision-making in particular is expensive to the brain, so these autopilot settings are helpful.

Impulse Purchases

An impulse purchase is a purchase that you didn't go to the store for, probably didn't want or need, and yet you bought it anyway. Retailers know that decision-making is expensive to the conscious brain, so they offer small things at the end of our shopping. This is the candy in the checkout aisle or the "users also purchased this" section. Impulse purchases are hard to avoid because your brain is already tired from making decisions and your impulse control is low. If you were shopping on autopilot, impulse purchases are invisible to the conscious brain at checkout.

Shop Big & Less Often

The principle I teach here is to shop less. The less you shop, the less you spend in terms of time, money, and energy. There are a few reasons this works so well. First, when you make a bigger purchase, the conscious brain gets involved so that you consider and make decisions more clearly. The less you shop, the less you expose yourself to a situation where you are making impulse purchases.

Jen is a big deal marketing director, while, at the time we worked together, her husband was a stay-at-home dad for their two-year-old.

Even though her husband was staying at home with their kid, she was still responsible for the shopping, money management, and most household stuff. As a result, she came to me feeling busy, broke, and exhausted . . . while making over $100,000 a year.

I asked her how much she thought she was spending a week on food, to which she guessed about $200 a week. When I dove into Jen's transactions, we found she was spending about $450 a week. This was because she was going grocery shopping five days a week, sometimes more.

It happened like this: She'd spend the first $200 in one big weekly shopping trip, then she'd spend an additional $250 weekly in three to five additional small trips. The small trips were always just for one or two things, but they would often cost $40–$80. This woman who was stretched for time, money, and energy was expending tremendous resources grocery shopping. Each of the trips was about an hour, totaling four to seven hours a week, along with the stress and mental load of additional tasks like remembering to run to the store for coffee.

So, we agreed to cut her shopping to once per week. This meant checking her house for her inventory before making a list. This step was missing before and was the cause of her forgetting one or two things. She committed to making do with what she had, so if she did forget something, she would work around it.

This change freed up twenty hours and $800 per month. She was able to use that money to pay for daycare for her toddler, which freed up her husband to go to work. She used the time to relax. She was able to declutter, clean, and organize her house. She ended the busy, broke, and exhausted cycle.

By evaluating your current shopping habits and implementing a system, you can drastically change your life. Here are my recommendations for how you should be shopping for common household items.

Food

Food is always one of the biggest areas of spending, which is normal and fine because we have to eat every day. Food is an area where time, money, and energy are all required. It is a place where we can spend a ton of money if we don't have time or energy to prepare meals. Many of my clients are spending much more on food than they would like.

As we move into this chapter, really understanding and considering time, money, and energy is the way to success.

Kirsta was spending about $1,500 per month on food, for her and her teenage son. She wanted to be spending $800. When we started working together, she was spending her entire Saturday going to three or four different grocery stores looking for the best deals. Then she didn't have time to rest or food prep. She works full-time and has heavy work responsibilities along with being a single mom. Many days after working and taking care of her son, she would go through the drive-through because cooking was daunting when she was low energy.

We started by changing her shopping habits to one trip to one store a week, with a monthly trip for bulk buys. Then she hired a local service for premade, healthy dinners to support her during the week. She has one night a week for dinner out with her son. These changes help her stick to her $800 per month grocery budget and have time to rest and play during the weekend.

Groceries

Declutter Your Kitchen
Clean out your pantry, cabinets, and freezer. Put anything expired on the counter so you can visually see the amount of kitchen clutter before tossing it. Notice how easy it is to see what you have when there is less. Food clutter creates wasted food, wasted money, and decision fatigue at cooking time.

Stick to a Schedule
Set a day of the week that you do your grocery shopping. This helps build a rhythm of food coming in, getting used, getting low, and being replenished. It creates a sense of safety to use all of your fresh food.

Set a Grocery Budget That Makes Sense
Few things cause ladies to self-torture like the grocery budget. Groceries are a nonnegotiable item yet

are adjustable. Look back through your transactions to total up the entire amount you spent on food. If you want to decrease the amount you spend on restaurants or takeout, you will likely need to increase the amount you spend on groceries.

If you are throwing away a lot of food, you can reduce your grocery budget. If you are not throwing much food away, there probably isn't room to cut your grocery budget. If your groceries are low at the end of the week and that causes you to buy takeout, you could increase your grocery budget.

Don't skimp on groceries, buy enough and get snacks and have some frozen meals for a day when fish sticks are just your best option. Get things you want to eat and enjoy. If you have teenagers, keep plenty of food they can feed themselves. Otherwise, they will harass you into trips to Taco Bell because there is no food at home. Skimping on groceries leads to additional trips to the store, stress, and unintentional takeout at the end of the week.

Plan Meals, Check Your Stores, and Make a List

Decide what you want to cook or eat next week. This helps you to make sure you have the right ingredients and don't have to make decisions and plans on weeknights when you are already tired.

Before you make your grocery list, check what you have. This helps you to avoid running out of something critical mid-week.

Truth & Grace
On Sunday morning, I am a domestic goddess, scrolling Pinterest for new recipes and planning meals with organic butternut squash. I have all the time in the world and sometimes bite off more than I can chew in the meal planning. On Tuesday night after I've worked all day, mothered the kids, and my stomach starts growling, I look at the penis-shaped squash on my counter and regret my choices.

The money-saving tips for saving money on groceries generally require more work, time, and energy. Things like, buy whole squash instead of chopped squash. Make your own pizza to save money. Consider whether you have the time and energy to spend before you save the money because throwing away food or ordering takeout is much more costly than getting the prepped veg.

Buy some frozen pizza or a Stouffer's lasagna to have on hand for a tough day.

One Store One Trip
One of the biggest ways clients overspend on groceries is by going to multiple stores. If you can get all of your groceries at one store, do it. I often hear concerns like the

snacks at Aldi are cheaper or Costco has better, cheaper something. Listen, I promise you it is cheaper to buy all the things at one store, in one trip. You use less time and gas and expose yourself to less impulse spending. Plus, if you only go to one store, you can spend the extra time on rest or food prep.

If you love to bulk shop, I suggest a trip once a month or once a quarter if that is possible for you. If you love different stores, rotate where you shop.

Using this strategy means getting resourceful. Going to the store for one or two things rarely works that way. If you have ever gone to the store for one thing, only to come out with a full basket and a $68 purchase, you know what I mean. If you forget something, do your best to work around it.

Delivery

This is one of my favorite recommendations, and it has transformed so many clients' lives. Try delivery or grocery pickup services. The delivery fee is usually a great deal compared to the gas, time, and mental energy that goes into shopping.

Grocery shopping online is an energy suck at first, but as the app learns your regular items, it gets faster and easier.

Adjust as Necessary

Notice what goes bad or doesn't get eaten and adjust spending as necessary. For a very long time, I threw away a bag of lettuce every week. I was attached to the idea of salads but didn't actually make them.

Takeout & Fast Food

Eating out is a wonderful experience for date nights, family dinners, birthdays, anniversaries, and catching up with friends. Eating out can also be a way that we invest in scarcity and spend a ton of money in ways that don't enhance our life. To be clear, before you make any adjustments to your spending on prepared food, evaluate whether it makes your life better. For example, my sister was visiting and we went out for dinner. We enjoyed the night, the food, and the service. The money I spent enhanced the quality of my life.

A different day, I worked late and waited until my kids were hungry to think about dinner, but by then I was exhausted and didn't want to cook. I ordered takeout to smooth out my life. While I am grateful to have the resources and service available, it's not a habit I want to build or a regular support I want to pay for.

How to Spend Less Eating Out

Evaluate the Habits and Add Supports

One of the clients I was working with has three kids. Every week, they spent $70 on takeout. $70 per week adds up. We're talking $3,640 per year. A lot of good can come from having that extra $70 each week to spend on something important.

To address this, we have to solve for the time crunch. She was buying takeout so she could use the time she would normally spend cooking to bathe the kids and help them with their homework. The solution we came up with was to use the times she did cook to make dishes that were easy to reheat. This way she would cook a double batch and freeze it. She'd also keep a few pizzas in the freezer.

She needed the time and energy of takeout to do other things. So we reorganized how she cooked so she could still have the time and energy to do what else she needed to do without spending the extra $70 per week. She had a time and energy problem that she tried to solve with money. But she could have it all. We have to plan for time, money, and energy.

If you find you need more time, consider meal delivery services. They might make more sense in your budget than you think, especially if they're an alternative to takeout. They look expensive compared to groceries, but they are often much cheaper than going out. Over the long run, you save time, money, and energy. In other words, you're reducing scarcity.

Look back at your transactions and look for habits and patterns around eating food. Make a list of the different habits and how much they cost and whether you want to keep them or change them.

Household Goods

Shop Once a Month to Once a Quarter

Beyond groceries, we need lots of other stuff to make our household go. For these kinds of shopping, I suggest taking inventory of what you use and how often. Keep a list and do your best to shop for toiletries, cleaning supplies, paper goods, home decor, etc. once a month. Big-box stores like Walmart and Target are the most deliciously convenient way to overspend.

Consider Online Alternatives

Can you find what you're looking for online instead of in-store? If so, check out services like Subscribe & Save or Target's Cartwheel. These services not only save money—both from the prices and avoiding impulse buys—but they also save a ton of time and mental energy. For my household, I get toilet paper through Subscribe & Save, and ever since I started the subscription years ago, I literally haven't thought about toilet paper since. It just shows up.

Online Shopping

Online shopping is gloriously convenient and magical. First, you can basically just put an idea into a Google search and the internet will magically connect you to a product. Then, you can buy it and a stranger in a brown van will just bring it to your house, no pants required. However, sometimes we get a little carried away with the magical convenience and highly targeted ads.

Save Your Amazon Purchases for Payday

Add things to your cart as necessary and hit the buy button on your payday. This helps you to see the total value of your spending in bigger increments. Generally, you will forget why you even wanted some of the things, so you can remove them. Plus adding things to your cart does offer a little dopamine release, so you still get some feel-good shopping. Don't wait on anything that's necessary or needed quickly.

Remove Your Cards from Your Phone or Browser

If online shopping is a problem for you, it is likely because you are buying things on autopilot and it all happens so fast. Taking the cards out of your browser or phone means you have to physically get up to get your card, and that is enough to break the spell of being on autopilot. It adds a slight inconvenience and time delay to the routine part of that habit and gives you a moment to consider with the conscious brain.

Don't Buy from Bed

Late-night scrolling is a surprisingly common way to spend a ton of money on stuff you didn't actually want. The ads are so targeted and have vast knowledge of your desires and patterns. When you are thinking about buying something, send yourself the link to the ad and look again the next day. When you are scrolling at night, you are generally spent for the day, on autopilot, and processing any emotions from the day. This is a perfect recipe for unwanted purchases.

Clothing Stores

Evaluate Your Wants/Needs

Before you even hit the store's parking lot, you want to know your needs. Take a peek in your closet, drawers, and storage bins. Lay out everything you either don't wear or that doesn't fit. Decluttering your closet is a great move once you have everything out to see. Once all of that's out, then take a look at what's left. Now, you have an accurate picture of what you need.

Shop Two to Four Times a Year

Shopping for clothes less often leads to less spending and a more cohesive wardrobe. Additionally when you take a substantial budget shopping, you can buy investment pieces that will look great for years to come. It is often enough to stay trendy.

Go Easy on Yourself

Changing your habits requires your brain to rewire itself. It takes a minute and conscious effort to effectively make changes. As you start this process, start with the lowest-hanging fruit and things that will have the most bang for your buck in terms of habit change to freed up cash flow. Celebrate all your wins, especially the small ones. Congratulate yourself on the progress you are making. Pat yourself on the back every single chance you get. This helps to build trust in yourself, and the more you trust yourself with money, the better your future decisions will be.

Avoid nit-picking and expecting perfection because that kind of mental behavior can suck the wind from your sails and derail your progress. Remember, you will have a relationship with money and spending every day of your life. It won't ever be perfect or perfectly under control and that is OK.

Emotional Spending

Jean was spending a lot of money on high-end makeup. I am talking the equivalent of thousands of dollars a year was ending up wasting away in drawers in her bathroom. She didn't even wear most of it. When we looked at this spending, she noticed she would often buy things when she was feeling down either at work or in the evening after a glass of wine.

We discussed what emotional need she was meeting through the spending, and we found she would buy makeup when she wanted to feel confident. The problem here is that new lipstick doesn't actually provide confidence. We discussed what it would actually take to feel confident, and she had a few things on that list that were big changes she wanted to make. She decided that she would stop drinking after work because it slowed her in the mornings and lowered her mood. She felt better when she took her dog for a walk in the morning. When she got up and moved her body, she went to work feeling confident.

Understanding Spending Habits

When you're looking to change your spending habits, look at your habits as a circle consisting of three things: **Trigger, Routine, Reward.**

Imagine you're on your way to work. On your route, you pass by a Starbucks and get a certain feeling. That's the **Trigger**.

Then, you decide to go through the drive-through because you deserve it. That's the **Routine**.

Finally, you swipe your credit card and put your hands on that sweet, hot caffeinated beverage, gloriously filling your heart and belly with delight. That's the **Reward**. The reward may be an emotional state or the avoidance of an emotional state.

This is a **habit loop**. Something triggers a desire to spend. A routine is created to satisfy that desire. You receive the reward that satisfies that desire. It's a cycle that keeps habits going forward.

Almost all spending has an emotional reward. Where emotional spending becomes problematic is when the routine we create with our habits does not fill the emotional need in a sustainable way. It forces us to get that need met over and over again, creating a financial problem.

The Truth about Habit Loops

Your brain builds habit loops to save itself from making decisions. The repetition helps your brain build a system for how to behave, which helps it conserve energy. When it comes to changing spending, there are a few important things to know.

First, it takes a tremendous amount of brain power to change a habit, so it's best to do one or two at a time. Changing too many habits at once will often fail, and it isn't because you lack willpower or suck at finances. It's because you asked your brain to do more than was reasonable.

Second, the reward needs to be addressed. Let's think about the coffee example for a moment. If I change the habit and make coffee at home, that is far more likely to work than going without coffee.

Identify the Trigger

Before you can address a habit loop, it is best to understand the trigger, routine, and reward. Triggers can be time, visual, emotional, or task-related. To change the habit loop, you have to identify the trigger. Sometimes triggers can be avoided; sometimes they can't.

Stephanie worked in a special needs classroom for kids with severe behavioral challenges. That job is stressful, and when one of her students had an intense behavior, she would buy something as she took a moment to regulate. For this client, the trigger was the student's behavior, the routine was the moment to breathe and hit "buy now," and the reward was the regulation and little dopamine hit. She actually didn't want the things she bought, and the little "presents" she bought herself were stressful.

Replace the Routine

Now that we've identified the trigger, we can replace the routine if necessary.

For Stephanie, we knew that her students would have behaviors and she needed a routine that would help her regulate. We tried a few different things, and what ended up working was stepping outside her classroom for a moment for a few deep breaths. The moment of downtime was an effective change because she did not want the items she was buying in a high-stress moment.

To effectively replace the routine, you need to understand what the real reward is. For Stephanie, we realized that buying wasn't the real reward—calming down was. Once she figured this out, deep breathing was a better routine.

Dee Dee was a client who was recently divorced and an empty nester. A few days a week, she would stop at the bar for chicken wings and beer. She would scroll on her phone while she waited and then go home. Her trigger for this habit loop was avoiding loneliness. The routine didn't fill that need very well, but it staved off the loneliness for a few hours and took the edge off. The reward wasn't filled all the way because she really wanted a higher quality social interaction. She put a plan in place to go to local meetup groups for real estate investors because she had a goal of buying a rental property. Within a year, she had new friends and an investment property.

Keep habits in mind as we move through the sections on freeing up cash flow. One of the biggest mistakes we make on our financial journey is only looking at the surface-level problems. When we keep an eye on our time and energy resources, in addition to our emotional needs, we can very quickly address the root cause of problems.

Spending your time, money, and energy is the creative magic of life—the exact place where your internal resources become your external life. Spending your resources with intention and regard for one another is incredibly helpful in money management that sticks and also in creating a beautiful existence. Most of the women I've worked with have tremendous mental and physical workloads; my hope is that you set realistic expectations for yourself.

Do the Work: Identify Waste

For this activity, identify waste in your transactions. To do this, grab your journal or notebook, pen, highlighters, and thirty days of transactions. Print out last month's bank statement(s). Track how often you are making purchases in each category of your personal finances. For example, write down the total of every food purchase you have made. Highlight them as you go. You may want to use a different color highlighter for each category. Include fast food, restaurants, snacks, and the grocery store. Count the total number of transactions you have made. Then, total up and write down the total amount spent. Finally, estimate the total amount of time you spent making these purchases. You can also find this activity in the companion workbook, which can be downloaded for free at https://www.cashconfidentbook.com/workbook.

Other categories to consider:
- Clothing
- Household Goods
- Gas Station/Convenience Store
- Online Shopping

Trigger, Routine, Reward

Look at your transactions through the lens of habits. To do this, start on a fresh page in your journal or notebook. Divide the page into three columns. Label the first column "Trigger," the second column "Routine," and the third column "Reward."

Next, all transactions including breakfast, coffee, lunch, dinner, cocktails, and date nights. Look for the habits that lead to these transactions. Break them down by their trigger, routine, and reward.

Here's an example:

Let's say I have a habit of buying coffee on my way to work. The trigger may be needing caffeine to start my day, or the sight of the Starbucks along my commute. The routine is going through the drive-through. The reward is the hot cup of coffee and glorious caffeine hitting my system.

Let's say I buy coffee while I am out with my friends. The trigger may be looking for connection and texting my friends to see whether they are around. The routine is meeting at the coffee shop. The reward is the connection with my friends.

In the first example, making coffee at home and bringing it to work gets the same glorious caffeine into my body. In the second example, the coffee was only a means for connection, and cutting it out in an attempt to save money will only work if that connection is found in another way, perhaps by meeting for a walk rather than a coffee date.

After completing this exercise, start to think about which habits need to change and how to get the reward in a better way. Consider which habit has the biggest impact on your finances and which habit would be the easiest to change. To avoid overwhelm and feelings of failure, you want to concentrate on only changing one habit at a time.

CHAPTER 5:

Sophisticated Spending

Linda and Lance had been putting the same family vacation to a lake cabin two towns over on their credit card for years, even though they'd tried to save the money. When we talked about this vacation, it was fairly clear they didn't actually want to go. A dusty cabin with the in-laws at a place they'd been a zillion times just wasn't exciting. They really wanted to go to Napa Valley, stay in a bougie hotel, and drink fancy wine. They thought, since they had trouble saving for the cabin, that it would be impossible to get to California. The thing is, they really wanted to go to Napa, so when it came time to make the small choices, the decision was clear. It took about a year to plan, schedule, and save for the trip, but they did it. That is the power of true desire and intentional spending at work.

In the last chapter, we tracked our money and freed up cash flow. This gives us the money we need to start building the life we want. In this chapter, we will look at how to use our money to create joy and satisfaction, while staying off the cycle of being busy, broke, and exhausted.

The Truth of Desire

Money is a tool for creation. We go to work to trade our time and energy for money. Then, that money can be traded into basically anything and any time. This is one of the reasons I love money so much; it is just magic. Using money to create a life we love is a delicious use of cash.

The first step of building a life you want is knowing the truth of what you want. This is a really important piece because trying to save or use money for big things that we don't actually want is difficult.

Desire is not a thing you "figure out." It is something you feel into. It is in the heart and intuition much more than the mind. Learning to listen to desire can be a small practice at first. Close your eyes for a moment and bring your attention to your heart. You can even put a hand on your heart. Ask yourself what you desire and be quiet to feel for the answer. It takes some practice. Start by listening for things like "What do I want to eat?" or "What do I want to do in this moment?" We are conditioned to mistrust and ignore desire, so it may take a few weeks to start to hear it. Desire drives growth and expansion.

Desire and Decision

One of the biggest holdbacks with time and money happens around the decision-making process. Often people want something, but it seems out of reach, and they wait until they have the money to decide whether they will get it. That doesn't work so well, and people can let years go by not getting what they want while they wait for money. There is a part of our brains called the reticular activating system (RAS), which is responsible for finding the opportunities and evidence. If you don't decide to do something, then that part of your brain doesn't get programmed to look for how to make it happen. When you decide that you will have your desire, the RAS starts looking for the ways and opportunities to make it happen.

Treasures and Trinkets

"I can't afford it" is one of the absolute worst things you can tell yourself about the things you want to have or create. First, it shuts down the brain from coming up with ways to get the things you want. Second, it creates smaller spending habits that use the resources you could use to get what you want. For example, you could spend $10,000 all at once or on a daily $27 purchase. When we try to keep spending in small increments, we often end up with trinkets instead of treasures. So don't say, "I can't afford this." Instead, ask yourself, "How can I afford this?"

The Myth of Needs and Wants

There is a myth or rather limiting belief that is widely accepted in the mainstream about spending money. The myth goes something like, it is OK to buy what you need but not what you want. Lots of parents even have this discussion with kids as a reason to decline a request. "You don't need that."

This belief causes a waste of mental energy, less satisfaction about spending, and less intentional spending overall.

When we need something, we are in the vibe of lack. You are probably reading this exact book to have more abundance and less lack in your life. When we get something we lack, it brings us back to normal, but it provides no upgrade.

When we believe that it is only OK to buy what we need, our mind has to turn wants into needs to justify making the purchase. The justification is a waste of mental energy that also reinforces the myth. Generally, we make the justification by degrading something we have, which creates even more lack. Then sometimes while we turn something into a need, we still can't justify spending on things we really want, so we buy something less expensive and lose satisfaction. When we make a want into a need, we miss all the upgrade vibes, all the luxury, because it just brings us back to normal. Also, we are much more likely to use credit to buy a need rather than delay the purchase to save the money. I'll tell you the same story two ways.

First story: I went to Tory Burch and fell in love with a purse that was beyond my budget for purses. I looked at my old purse, and even though it was a nice quality, it was old. The bottom was scuffed and it was worn out. I decided I needed a new purse to replace the old purse. I couldn't justify spending a lot of money on the Tory Burch bag, so I went to Marshalls and bought a bag I didn't really want to satisfy the need. I didn't like the new bag, so I went back to Tory Burch and bought the bag I wanted.

Second story: I went to Tory Burch and fell in love with a purse that was beyond my normal budget for purses. I looked at my old purse, which was seven years old and still in great shape. I decided to save the money for the new bag. I was excited and anticipating the new bag while I saved the money. When I wear the new bag, it feels abundant and luxurious.

When we look at the feelings underneath each story, they are very different. The first story starts with a desire that turns to lack, degradation, and dissatisfaction. I end up with a bag that I don't even really desire, just to satisfy a need. Then I feel guilty for buying two.

The second story also starts with a desire but follows with gratitude and acknowledgment, then anticipation, accomplishment, satisfaction, and luxury. See the difference?

The way we feel about money, spending, and purchases colors the fabric of our lives. You always want to take care of your actual needs before buying things you want. This is important to create a sense of safety within yourself and, you know, be a responsible adult. Once you have what you need, buying what you want just because you want it without need for justification creates a much more abundant feeling in your life.

The Myth of "I Can Do It All"

Spend on Higher Levels of Support

Women today are producing what took two people fifty years ago. We are generally working full-time, mothering the kids, pets, and plants, keeping a clean house, working out, staying hydrated, and being a sex goddess. It is overwhelming. Often we use money to pick up the slack, but not always to buy the highest level of support possible. Most of the women I've worked with resist paying for support because they are capable of doing things on their own.

Take a look at your life and the places you may require an extra hand. Look for the places when time gets tight or energy is depleted and think about how to use your money to buy the highest level of support. I suggest using the information you gathered about your spending habits to look at how much you are spending on takeout food, convenience purchases, and anything else that provides Band-Aid support.

I mentioned a story about a client who was buying more than $1,000 in prepared foods every month. Those purchases helped her with time and energy, but they were the lowest level of support, a Band-Aid instead of what she really needed. The food was junk and required more time and energy. She replaced those purchases with using a service that made healthy and delicious dinners to keep in the freezer. This is a higher level of support, meaning fewer trips to the drive-through and higher quality of food. There was even enough for her to pack for lunch the next day. In this case, the higher level of support was less expensive than all the trips through the drive-through.

Prioritizing rest and rejuvenation is important to have the energy required to maximize earning potential and enjoy life. Meal services, housekeeping, or laundry services are all worthwhile spending when done intentionally.

Intentional Emotional Spending

Almost all spending is emotional spending. Turning your money into things you need or want is a creative process and emotions play an important role. Unintentional emotional spending will have you leaking cash flow, chasing your tail, and overspending. But when you are clear about what emotional states you want to create with your money, you can be much smarter.

A client was a nurse who had Tuesdays off. On Tuesdays, most of her friends were working and so was her spouse. On Tuesdays she would get bored, want to feel productive, and head out shopping. It wasn't the need or desire for more home decor driving this; it was boredom and wanting to feel productive. The shopping would give her a reason to leave the house, but then she had to deal with the clutter and credit card bills. Once she realized she was bored and wanting to feel productive, she was able to adjust her behavior to meet that need. She added hikes and visits to see her grandmother to her Tuesday routines because both got her out of the house and allowed her to feel productive, without the clutter or credit cards.

When you think about what emotional state you are buying with a purchase, you can better gauge whether that purchase is a good way to fill that need, and you may also see other ways to get that need met that don't cost money.

One day I was having a long day and a rough week, and I really wanted to eat crunchies while telling my dear friend about the ridiculousness of my existence. The things I really wanted were connection and conversation, but I was going to invite her out for dinner and drinks. However, there were other options. For example, I could pick up some wine, cheese, and crackers and head to her house or call her on the phone to meet the same need. This doesn't always work, but when you are habitually spending money on the same emotional need, it is worth looking at it on a deeper level. You might discover some great alternatives.

Sometimes looking at the emotional level of spending will point you to other changes that need to be made for fuller life happiness. Spending your money on purpose helps to create the life you want.

Money is a magical tool for life creation; you can turn money into literally anything. Spending your money, time, and energy with intention and direction is the key to power in your relationship with money. These ideas will help you to stop the flow of money from the things you don't want to fund, start the flow toward things you do want to fund, and slow the flow for big important things.

Do the Work: How to Recognize Desire

Start by finding a comfortable place to sit. Then, I want you to feel into your biggest desire. Feel it in your body. Notice the sensations. Feel how it tingles, burns, and vibrates within you.

Ponder on this desire a little more. Use your journal or notebook to write out what you want to create with your life force. What do you want to get out of it? This is a big, burning desire.

Next, feel into something you want, but I don't want it to be a soul-led desire. This is going to be something a little less desired than the one above. As you feel into it, I want you to notice the sensations in your body. This is a small to medium desire.

Finally, feel into something you do not want. This is something undesirable to you. Notice the sensation in your body.

At the end of this exercise, you will know what true desire feels like.

Now that you understand what desire feels like. I want you to take this a step further. Write down a desire that you have and answer the following questions. You can also find this activity in the companion workbook, which can be downloaded for free at: https://www.cashconfidentbook.com/workbook.

1. What do you want the process of fulfilling this desire to feel like?
2. What do you want to create, or how do you want to serve?
3. When you imagine this desire fulfilled, what feelings come up in your body?

Use this exercise to determine what you truly desire to spend your money on. When you understand what you truly desire, it becomes easier to spend your money intentionally.

CHAPTER 6:

Drop the Debt, Once and For All

Janie came to see me with $43,000 in credit card debt and feeling totally defeated. She has four children and had just reentered the workforce to pay for the kids' college. She and her husband were pulling in about $140,000 a year, which is a decent salary for where they live.

When I examined her spending, I found the issue: Janie was working three lower-paying jobs to pay off her credit card debt. She'd throw all of her money at the debt, which resulted in her having to use the credit card once she inevitably ran out of spending money.

Her plan was to "spend less," but her debt continued to grow every month.

Time was also an issue, and as we've seen in previous client stories, we often spend more money to make up for the loss of time. But if every dollar being made is put toward our debt, and all of our time is put toward making the money to pay off the debt, when it comes time to make normal everyday purchases, they often become an emergency that results in even more debt.

It's a vicious cycle and why I often compare it to a hamster wheel.

After a deep conversation with me, Janie realized that she was always in reaction mode. She had no plan and would try to work harder to make up for the extra expenses. Janie was busy, broke, and exhausted with the whole situation.

Here's how we solved it: First, I told Janie to literally freeze her credit cards. I'm not kidding. I had her go and get herself a Tupperware container, put the cards inside, fill it with water, and place it in the freezer.

Then, Janie gave her kids responsibility for their own expenses (car insurance, repairs, and the like) as well as boundaries around their daily expenses.

Eighteen months later, Janie and I met up at an event. She had nearly paid off her debt, had $10,000 in the bank, and had her first $18,000 month in her real estate business. Her husband (never met this guy in my life) came to see me just to give me a hug and tell me that my guidance helped them stop fighting. Janie finally understood her debt and took action.

The underlying habit of debt is feeling that you don't have money. Instead of addressing this habit, it's easier to put it on credit. Then, once you have more cash flow to use, it's even easier to throw it at the debt. That feels good . . . but it never addresses the habit that got you into debt in the first place. Welcome to the hamster wheel: paying off debt, not changing the habit, getting into debt, paying off debt, repeat.

If you have debt and some cash flow, you might focus all your free cash flow and attention on paying off debt. While that's natural, you're not saving.

How'd I Get Here?

Getting into credit card debt is easy to do. There are tons of options to help you spend money, including credit cards, offers like Klarna or Afterpay, personal loans, 401(k) loans, etc. The first step in getting out of consumer debt permanently is to evaluate what got you there in the first place. The purpose of this kind of evaluation is to point your efforts in the right direction.

Once I had a client who was blaming her student loan payments for all sorts of financial malady, but when we looked deeper, we found her savings habits were nonexistent, so even if her student loan disappeared, the root of her debt would still be there.

It's Probably Not Irresponsible or Reckless Overspending

One of the biggest myths about credit card debt is that it is the result of irresponsibility or recklessness. The truth is most people don't recklessly spend. After working with so many people, I've found that most credit card debt doesn't come from luxury vacations or shopping sprees. In reality, it comes from a lack of clarity, lack of preparation, and inadequate savings habits.

For example, if you own a house, you know you'll have to replace your water heater one day. Maybe that day is fifteen years from now or tomorrow, but that day will come no matter what. Being prepared with awareness and cash for these kinds of things prevents many unpleasant surprises.

Unclear Desires

If you don't know the truth of what you're trying to create with your money, it is easy to want everything. Every little gadget and course on Instagram will look shiny to you. You'll buy a little of everything, trying to satisfy your desire, but it won't last long. But when you're clear about your desires, you're better at avoiding spending money on things you don't actually want. It makes all of the temptations less shiny. Let's just say you get invited on a trip you really want to go on, and you recognize that every time you buy a little something here and there, it's less you can save for the trip. The clarity of desire creates something you check your wants against. Do I want this quesadilla or do I want to keep the $15 for my trip is a better question than quesadilla or no quesadilla.

Unclear Money Systems

I was working with a client whose debt had grown substantially since the last time she'd paid off a large balance and she couldn't understand why. When I looked at her money, I couldn't figure it out either. She had around ten bank accounts and a dozen credit cards, and she was shuffling her money through these accounts like a three-card monte. Since she was using credit cards, the time she had between the overspending and the realization was more than a month apart. Her system was so convoluted that she had no idea what money was going where, why, or when to stop spending.

Unclear Preparations

Staying out of credit card debt requires being prepared for things like taxes, snow tires, and wedding gifts. When we are so busy trying to make ends meet in the day-to-day, it is hard to bring our attention into the future to see what expenses are coming down the pike. Getting clear on big expenses coming in the next twelve months is critical to staying out of consumer debt. When we are unprepared for the things we need, using credit becomes necessary to keep afloat.

No or Low Savings Habits

The cause of debt is almost always needing money. The solution to needing money is having money. We build the ability to have money by building savings habits. It is best to have three separate savings habits for what I call Planting, Preparing, and Pleasure. I want to stress the importance of these savings as habits, not just money in an account. It is the perpetual replenishment of these funds as they get used that is critical.

Low Comfort Zone Around Savings

A client of mine usually had only a few hundred to $2,000 in her savings account. She got a tax refund of $14,000 and put it in her savings account. That cash on hand would have helped her get a step ahead in her financial plans and have the security to stay out of credit card debt, but the money freaked her out and she got rid of it. Staying out of debt requires us to get used to having money and letting that money chill out in our bank account.

Underearning

Underearning is when your earnings don't match your potential or desires. It often causes credit card debt because there is not enough money to cover the necessities, or there is just enough to survive but not enough to enjoy. Once I had a client who was in the same job for thirty years, and her budget was dialed in. She knew where every dollar was going, and there was nothing frivolous in her budget. She wanted to be able to take a trip once a year, but the math wouldn't work on paper. Her salary had increased with the cost of living over the years, but she wasn't earning enough to have any money for pleasure. When debt is caused by underearning, the solution has to include an earnings piece.

Drop the Debt, Once and For All

The Hamster Wheel of Debt

The hamster wheel of debt goes something like this: accrue debt, use all your free cash flow to pay off debt, life gives you a surprise expense, use credit to pay for the expense because you don't have any cash on hand, repeat. Sometimes the wheel of debt gets bigger, especially when we borrow money to pay back borrowed money while keeping the habits and mindsets that caused us to borrow money in the first place.

Getting off the hamster wheel once and for all requires changing the mindsets and habits that caused the debt in the first place. The suggestions below may seem slower than you might like because you are building the habits to make a permanent change in your relationship with consumer debt.

Step One: Change Your Habits (Months 1 through 3)
You may find this part frustrating. You may overdraw your account. That's normal. Think of it this way: Your money used to feel like yoga pants (infinitely stretchy and forgiving), but now you're working with jeans. Be patient.

Once you decide to get out of credit card debt once and for all, take the first few months to adjust your cash flow and habits to accommodate the changes. Give yourself time to adjust and get good with the change.

1. Stop Using the Cards
Remove your cards from your wallet, digital wallet, or browser. If you need to, literally freeze your cards in Tupperware in the freezer. This sounds crazy, but trust me, it works for a lot of people because it adds a layer of conscious choice and a small time delay. If you do need to get the cards, run the ice under hot water; don't use the microwave. Leave your accounts open.

2. Pay Only the Minimums on the Cards

It may sound counterintuitive, but paying only the minimum on your cards will allow you to get used to a tighter cash flow. It will leave some room to start building your savings so you can focus on becoming the person who has money, not just someone who pays off debt. Slow and steady wins the race.

I get pushback from clients when I suggest they pay only the minimum amount. If your cash flow is strong, then you can go ahead and start with a debt payment higher than the minimum. Just be sure you are able to save money habitually.

3. Forget About Credit Card Points

Credit card companies get paid on transaction fees and on interest. The transaction fees are invisible to the consumer, but when you use your card, the processing costs about 3 percent, which is paid by the business. Credit card companies have worked diligently to make their cards more and more convenient, and even incentivize using cards all the time with points. This is a wildly lucrative strategy for them, but it is incredibly damaging to most people's habits.

While you're paying off debt and securing your financial future, credit card points are only a distraction. I suggest using cards for the points once you have three to six months of cash in the bank, and not before. If you pay interest on a balance, it very quickly wipes out any value added by the points.

4. Celebrate
Keep a victory journal to track every win and triumph. This step is crucial for noticing trends, correcting mistakes, and maintaining your momentum.

5. Repeat After Me
Repeat the following mantras.

"It doesn't have to be perfect to be progress."

"There is no such thing as perfect finances. You are human."

"Focus on the eight things you did well today, not the two things you could have done better."

Step Two: Learn How to Have Money & Reframe Your Mindset
When we're talking about having money, you may remember I mentioned three types of savings habits you should have.

Planting: Long-term savings for your future. Investments, nest eggs, etc.

Preparing: Medium-term savings for normal purchases and emergencies. Car repairs, house upgrades, needed vacations, and so on. I call this type of savings Working Capital.

Pleasure: Short-term savings to enjoy your life and make upgrades.

It's important to define what each one looks like for you and enjoy all three.

Money habits take longer to build than most habits because most only get two opportunities per month. In chapter 7, we go into more detail on how to build a money management system.

Set up those three savings habits, and learn to save while stretching your financial comfort zone. Stay with these habits for a minimum of three months before choosing a strategy. While you are working this part of your plan, start working on your money mindset.

Reframe Your Mindset

I think it's important to challenge our mindset around interest, spending money, and debt. There's so much emotion and judgment around these subjects, which can shame people out of taking action and encourage bad habits. In addition, people worry that imperfection is a sign they're headed in the wrong direction. Let's address these myths and reframe them:

Interest Is Not a Scam

Interest is the price you pay to have access to a purchase before you can afford it. When people see interest as a scam, it creates resentment toward the credit card and, in general, frustration around money, none of which is helpful toward straightening out your finances. When we feel like we're getting screwed, it creates this resistance that keeps us from wanting to pay it back. This resistance makes it hard, even painful, to let go of the money.

Mental Chatter Tells You Where Your Comfort Zone Is
As you embark on this journey, you may find your mind to be piping up more than usual. You may find your mental chatter gets louder and louder, to the point where you start wondering whether you're doing something wrong. You're not. Chatter doesn't mean your plan isn't working—it means your comfort zone is stretching. And when your comfort zone stretches, that's when self-sabotage shows up. So if your mind is chattering away, stick to your plan.

A client saved $10,000 in her savings account. All this money had a purpose and would be used in the next twelve months, but that extra zero put her beyond her comfort zone. Her brain bothered her for weeks until it got used to having that much money. Her brain was bothering her by constantly bringing up all the things she could do with the money. She could pay off a credit card, she could buy a new couch, the list went on and on. She stuck with her plan and stretched her comfort zone.

Step Three: Choose Your Strategy

Before you choose a strategy, make sure you change your habits and mindset first. If you skip those steps, your old spending habits will come roaring back. It'll take a few months to get used to your new habits and mindset without a credit card getting involved, so be patient.

Once you have changed your habits and reframed your mindset, it's time to take action. You're ready to pay off debt and be financially free, and there's more than one way to do it. Each strategy has its pros and cons, depending on your situation. I'll lay them out and give you my honest take on each.

Before I do, here's how you know you're ready to pick a strategy:
1. You haven't used your credit card in three months.
2. You have at least one month of expenses saved.
3. You have extra money going toward minimum payments.

1. The Snowball

List out your credit cards from smallest to biggest balance, irrespective of interest rates. Set yourself a total debt payment amount that would consist of the total of the minimum payments plus any additional money to put toward debt. Then, you pay the minimums on all of your cards except for the smallest one. All the extra money you have to pay down your debt goes to the smallest debt. When that's paid off, you "snowball" the money originally going toward the previous smallest debt now toward the next smallest debt. There's some mental satisfaction in this strategy because you pay off cards faster, and it can be effective if you have a lot of small credit cards or loans.

2. The Avalanche

The avalanche strategy uses the same idea as the snowball, but instead of prioritizing the smallest debt amount, you prioritize the highest interest rate. The idea is that, by eliminating high interest rates, you're saving more money in the long run. I've worked with some folks who pull their hair out when they think of paying high interest rates, so if that's you, the avalanche is a formidable pick.

3. Snowball with Credit Card Shuffle

As the name suggests, the snowball with credit card shuffle strategy is identical to the snowball plus one extra step. The idea is to move a high interest rate debt (a credit card) to a lower interest one, typically a new credit card with a 0 percent interest rate, to reduce your overall monthly interest expense. I totally get the idea behind this, and if doing this gives you peace of mind, then go for it.

Warning: Change your habits first. The risk of this method is you are taking out new credit, so if you haven't addressed your habits, there's a very big risk that you will increase the size of your credit card problem in a couple of years.

4. 401(k) Loan

A 401(k) loan is sometimes an option when people have super tight cash flow. If your debt is so big that you are unable to save or do other things, a 401(k) loan might be an option. If so, you need to run the numbers to make sure that it has the impact you want, including freeing up cash flow. The upside is it's your money and you pay it back to yourself. The downside is that, if you lose your job, you need to pay it back right away or you end up getting taxed as an early distribution. Another downside is it takes money out of the stock market, and you lose that growth.

These loans tend to offer a lower interest rate than credit cards (but check to make sure), and you get to just pay it back via payroll deduction, so it's relatively simple to administer. However, because you're paying it back from payroll deduction, it also lowers your paycheck, so make sure the amount you will be saving in payments to your credit cards is greater than the decrease in your paycheck or you will end up with even worse cash flow.

Finally, once your cards are paid off, you remain at risk of getting back into debt and having both a 401(k) loan *and* new credit card debt. I recommend making sure you've changed your habits to not use credit cards for at least six months so you are more comfortable that your habits have changed.

5. Personal Loan

Personal loans serve the same purpose as 401(k) loans and carry most of the same risks. You go to the bank and take out a loan to pay off your credit cards. This helps consolidate your debts into one payment, can lower interest rates, and reduces the mental space needed to maintain multiple debt accounts. But, like with other consolidation options and 401(k) loans, if you haven't changed your habits, it's not a great solution.

6. Debt Consolidation

There are services that generally close your accounts, negotiate your interest rates down to 0 percent, and administer the paydown. Often, you pay them every month and they pay the credit card company for a period between three and seven years. These services make me leery, as I've heard some horror stories. Plus, the method destroys your credit, and it takes a long time to get back into good standing. It's often better to just file for bankruptcy protection if you're in that deep of a mess and have no other options.

7. Bankruptcy

Bankruptcy is not my favorite recommendation to give. Not only is it an extreme solution but it also comes with a lot of emotions, including shame and embarrassment. When the balance on consumer debt is higher than six months of income, that is when I start considering bankruptcy. If you think you might be to the point where you don't have options, consult with a bankruptcy lawyer to understand how it will impact you. Sometimes it is the best solution. For example, I worked with a lady whose husband passed away and she could not manage her debt load and take care of her kids on her own. For her, after talking with a bankruptcy attorney, the best option turned out to be filing for bankruptcy protection. But oftentimes, you have other options.

Debt is probably the biggest financial thorn for people, and it's a major reason for financial suffering. Taking a slower approach that gives time to build and break habits is far more effective than rushing. As you make changes and pay off your debts, make sure to pat yourself on the back.

In the next chapter, we will get into how to systemize your money to really solidify getting out of debt, once and for all.

Do the Work: Root Causes of Debt

Before we begin, I want you to tally all your debts. Open up to a blank page in your journal or notebook. Divide the page into five columns. Label each column as follows: Account Name, Balance Owed, Minimum Payment Due, Payment You Make, and Interest Rate. Fill the columns out accordingly for each of your debts. This will give you clarity on what you owe and how much you are paying in interest. The information will help you choose a strategy for paying off the debt. You can also find this activity in the companion workbook, which can be downloaded for free at https://www.cashconfidentbook.com/workbook.

Next, I want you to identify the root causes of your debt. Turn to a blank sheet of paper in your notebook or journal. Take notes on how each of the following shows up for you.

Unclear Desires
- Lack of awareness around money
- Unrealized unhappiness
- Using money as a stress reliever

Unclear Money Systems
- Unsure what money is coming in or going out
- Confusing money system for checking, savings, and credit card accounts

Unclear Preparations
- No understanding of what expense is coming
- No habitual savings for necessities

No or Low Savings Habits
- Low comfort zone for savings
- No savings habit in place

Low Comfort Zone around Savings
- Feel uncomfortable when money accumulates
- Spend money because it's uncomfortable to keep in the bank

Underearning
- Earnings don't match potential or desire
- Unable to ask for a raise or feel stuck in a position or salary level

Then, consider how you are going to address your debt. Take a moment to write about it in your journal or notebook. What approach will you take? What habits will you change? Can you identify any focus or mindsets that caused the debt or will need to change?

Finally, write a letter to your debt thanking it for how it has served you. We tend to carry negative energy, shame, and judgment around our debt, but I want you to remember that access to credit served you. Have gratitude and appreciation for the debt. Tell it that you appreciate it has been there for you when you needed it most. Let the shame and judgment go.

CHAPTER 7:

The Invisible System

Melissa and her husband, two brilliant people, came to me with the hottest mess of a financial situation I'd ever seen. They didn't have a clue what to do with their financial situation. At first, I was surprised because they sounded like they had a pretty solid foundation when I spoke to them. She had a master's degree while he worked as an incredible tradesman and made great money. Despite all that education and skill, they told me something was wrong with their finances. So, I took a look.

Melissa and her husband kept one account for everything . . . and I mean everything. They each had a debit card for the accounts. No one knew what money went where, bills weren't paid on any type of a schedule, and no one knew which bills were paid versus unpaid. The bills were often paid late, causing fees and the threat of losing service.

This one-account "system" led to constant overdraft fees, stress, and bickering. They were fighting because they could see every transaction the other one made and because they were out of cash with obligations still due. It resulted in each of them blaming the other because of where they were spending.

To make matters worse, their credit was also a hot mess, and they were in a bad rental situation. They wanted to buy a house but were not able to save a down payment, and their credit score reflected mismanagement.

We started working together by adding a system to their money so they could start making progress toward their dream house. Money does require your attention for a continued good relationship, but when you have a system built, it is so much easier to maintain than a budget or plan.

Let me introduce the Invisible System. It is a no-budget system to manage household finances. This is the exact way I've taught thousands of clients to manage their money. It manages money so well because it is a system rather than a plan. When the system is set up, it provides clarity of finances, uses technology to support good habits, and centralizes banking, bill payments, and savings. In this chapter, I will explain the big-picture system, and in the next, we will get a little more into the nitty-gritty of how to build it out for yourself.

There are some major benefits to setting up the Invisible System:

Reduces the Mental Load of Household Money Management

Money management, when done well, is basically invisible, but it requires a lot of mental energy to track money, pay the bills on time, reduce debt, and save for important things. This system helps to reduce that load by using technology to systemize cash flow and bill payments. In time, you can reduce your money management to about thirty minutes a month for tracking, bill payment, and investment management.

Maintains Clarity

Most people overspend accidentally because they lack clarity on what money is available to spend and what money in their account is essentially already spent. Setting up the Invisible System separates your money by purpose. When you log into your account, you will look at one account to know how much money you can spend between now and your next paycheck. Of course, the money is yours, and you can move it if necessary, but you will do it on purpose with clarity.

Uses Technology to Support the Good Habits

Saving money is psychologically tough to do. Every time we have to save, our brain will consider all the things we could be doing with the money, and since the subconscious part of your brain—the part motivated by sex and snacks—is really running the show, savings can be put off month after month. Automating your savings habits while doing your bill pay manually works in your favor by keeping your eyes and decision-making on the outflows, while the cash stacks up automatically.

Keeps You Off the Plastic

Being prepared by funding a "Working Capital" account is the best way to stay out of credit card debt, get good at having bigger sums of money, and reduce the number of money emergencies. This is the heart of the Invisible System. Many people I have talked to look at their monthly expenses and plan for those, but they forget to plan for semiannual and annual expenses, turning expected expenses into "emergencies," for things like new tires or brakes for the car. A Working Capital account takes these expenses into consideration when setting aside money on payday.

Takes the Important Things into Consideration

The entire reason you would ever make a plan, set a budget, or build a system is to be able to buy a better life for yourself. When we don't have good control over our money, these are the things that may be pushed aside because we "can't afford it." Planning out and setting aside funds for travel, renovations or big lifestyle upgrades is important because it is essentially the payoff for doing all this work to change our habits and mindset.

Before Melissa and her husband worked with me, they believed that if their income was good, they'd automatically have money left over at the end of the month and, like magic, money would suddenly appear in their savings.

Once we implemented the Invisible System to their money, Melissa and her husband had savings for the first time in their midforties. They had retirement money. Their bills finally got paid on time. Money management became easy and clear. They both had spending money they could use without a fight.

Within a year and a half, they were even able to get out of their rental, buy a house, and find peace with their money.

So if you feel like your finances are a hot mess, I'll show you the same system I used to give Melissa and her husband control over their money, help them reach life goals, and finally create peace of mind around money. I call it the Invisible System because, once you get it going, it'll run in the background while you live your life.

How to Start Building Your System

One of the biggest problems with budgets is that there are often more than one hundred moving line items. This creates the need for constant tracking, adding to the mental load. Plus, when the tracking isn't up to date, you are budget blind.

In the Invisible System, we use the Five Types of Money. These Five Types of Money each have a purpose, rhythm, habit, and account. Separating the money by purpose helps to maintain clarity so you can look at your bank account and instantly know where you stand financially. There are three types of savings and two types of spending that we will go over now.

1. Investment

The purpose of investing money is to invest, grow, and produce lots of baby money to provide cash flow for you to live on. This is the first place you want your money to go because paying yourself first sends a message to your subconscious that you are your top priority. Energetically, this money attracts more and more money. Plus, you are buying yourself freedom from work because once this money produces enough cash flow to cover your living expenses, your time is set free.

For most people, their investment account will likely be a retirement account. Retirement accounts include a workplace plan like a 401(k), 403(b), 457, or

SIMPLE plan. Or you could have a personal retirement account like an IRA or a Roth IRA. If you have a business, you could use a Solo 401(k) or SEP IRA. Even real estate can be held for retirement in a self-directed IRA, although that is a more complex investment style. If you have access to a workplace plan for retirement, generally that is the easiest option to get started. You can also meet with a local investment advisor or with an online brokerage firm.

A good rule of thumb is to invest 10 percent of your income. If you can't start with 10 percent, just get started with what you can and increase your savings a little bit more every quarter.

The rhythm of this money is one big arc over your working lifetime. You save and invest from when you start working until your retirement. Then the money from your retirement investments covers expenses for the rest of your life.

2. Bills & Regular Monthly Expenses

The purpose of bills money is to pay your monthly bills and regular monthly expenses. This is the second place your money will go because taking care of our needs, before we plan for luxury or upgrades, creates a sense of safety and trust with money.

You will use a checking account for this. You want to look for a bank that has an online banking system so that you can pay all your bills digitally from your bank account. For convenience purposes, you want to have a debit card for this account.

I suggest using an online banking system to pay all the bills for a few reasons. First, it is easy and clear, not requiring spreadsheets, binders, or old shoe boxes full of statements. Online banking systems keep you organized and in a place where you can see all the bills being paid from which paycheck. Second, it keeps you looking at your money; often when bills are paid automatically, we miss errors or price increases. Once your online system is set up, paying all your bills takes about five minutes per month.

This number is customized to your exact expenses. Look back at your transactions and total up the cost of all your bills and expenses that happen monthly. Remember to include your subscriptions like Netflix and anything else that's automatically paid by your debit card. Make notes about the payment due dates.

Next, we are going to look at your nonnegotiable expenses that will go into your Pocket Money account. Total up your gas, groceries, childcare, transportation, or other essential weekly or monthly spending that you would pay for with cash or a debit card. This number will be allocated to your Pocket Money account, but we will reserve the cash now.

The rhythm of this money is a quick in and out on each payday. Every time you get paid, money will flow into this account, and then almost immediately it will go to pay your living expenses.

3. Working Capital

This is the magic sauce of the Invisible System—staying out of credit card debt and feeling at peace with your money. The purpose of this money is to be prepared for your financial needs that are coming up in the next twelve months. Saving money is a habit that you will continue. This helps you to build trust in yourself and your money and reduces financial stress by a ton.

It is worth noting that it is not an emergency fund, even though it can certainly be used for emergencies. When people save for emergencies, it creates more stress in their financial life because something needs to be an emergency to use the money.

Ever save $1,000 only to have it wiped out for a car repair? Most people pick a number to save for an emergency, then stop saving once they get there. When the emergency happens, they find themselves back at zero needing to rebuild the savings habit once again. This causes all sorts of emotional turmoil. Saving habitually to be prepared will help you to reduce the number of emergencies you have.

Working Capital is a savings account. You want to choose a savings account that has easy transfer access to your other accounts like your Bills or Pocket Money accounts. This makes it easy to use the money when the time comes. You want to be able to see this account when you log on online.

The amount that you will need to save in this account will be a best guess or projection of your expenses. This number will never be perfect because you are predicting the future, but with time, you can get closer and closer to knowing how much you need.

You want to think about all your irregular expenses—things like annual, semiannual, quarterly, and seasonal expenses. A good example is home and car insurance or HOA fees. These are things we often pay every six to twelve months. Also consider things such as regular car maintenance, like oil changes and wiper blades, or necessary replacement of goods. These are expenses that we can anticipate but often overlook when creating a plan for our money.

Also look at foreseeable disasters, like your car making weird noises, your dog's love affair with dangerous porcupines, insurance deductibles, doctor's bills—all things you know will happen at some point. List out family obligations, such as birthdays, parties or holidays you host, weddings, and back-to-school shopping. Finally, list out nonmonthly self-care like massages or

Botox and your twice-a-year clothing purchases, shoes, etc. The more you prepare, the more in control you'll feel of your money.

The rhythm of this money is less regular. Money will go into this account from each paycheck and will come out as necessary. Sometimes there will be quite the stockpile of cash, and other times the outflows will be more than the inflows. This account requires more emotional intelligence than the others. Many clients start to get attached to their money as it stockpiles and feel a sense of loss when they use it on the exact things they saved it for.

4. Important Things

Many people love the pleasure category because it involves things we actually like to spend money on. I call these the "Important Things." The purpose of saving this money is for upgrades to your lifestyle. Vacations, home upgrades, or other big one-time purchases are common uses of this type of money.

You will use a savings account for this. I generally suggest using the same bank for your whole system, although some people prefer to use a separate bank for this type of money so they don't feel tempted to use it on beer and peanuts.

You will calculate the cost by looking at the cost of the thing you want and the time frame you want it in.

For example, if you wanted a $1,200 weekend getaway twelve months from now, you would save $100 per month or $50 per paycheck (assuming biweekly paychecks). This makes saving for the pleasures that make life fun much more feasible.

When you see how much cash flow is available after you take care of your needs, then you can direct what is left to what you want.

5. Pocket Money

The purpose of pocket money is to spend within your pay period and then replenish. This money will be used for necessities like gas and groceries and for spending money on snacks and fancy gel pens. There are benefits to keeping all the money that will be spent separate. First, you will clearly be able to see how much money you have to spend between now and your next paycheck when you log in to your bank account. That clarity will give you the ability to make decisions.

Sometimes clients are tempted to not have any spending money and use all the cash flow toward debt. That is not effective. Restriction with spending money creates future binges, so you want to make sure you are able to indulge some of your small desires on a daily basis.

You will use a checking account with a debit card for this account. When the time comes to buy clothes or pay for other nonmonthly self-care, you will transfer the money from Working Capital to this account and use your debit card or cash to actually purchase the item.

This money is designed to run out between paychecks and then get replenished with your next paycheck. You will likely spend this money until it's gone because that is the nature of this type of account.

If you have a spouse or partner, they will want to have their own separate Pocket Money account. The separate accounts are easier to keep track of and reduce unsexy marital communication like, "Hey babe, can I buy a sandwich?" Rather than splitting the money equally, you will want to base the amount in those accounts on the needs of the situation. For example, if one partner is responsible for the household grocery shopping, their Pocket Money account will have significantly more in it than the other partner's.

Note: The Working Capital fund is always going to be more than you would think, and the Pocket Money fund is often less than you'd like.

Prioritize

In the Invisible System, accounts are funded in order of priority. This is important to create a sense of safety and energetic alignment for money manifestation.

First, we plant our money in an investment. This follows the old proverb "Pay yourself first." Paying yourself first is important because it sends a signal to your subconscious that if you value and take care of yourself, you will be rewarded for any additional work you do.

Second, we take care of our immediate needs with our Bills and Pocket Money accounts. This looks like paying your monthly bills and funding your Pocket Money account for the essentials like gas and groceries.

Third, we save money in preparation for the things we will need in the next twelve months in our Working Capital account. This requires us to project our needs in the future. This money helps us be ready for big expenses while staying out of debt.

Fourth, we save money for the pleasures in life. We calculate the cost of future travels or upgrades and set that money aside to accumulate.

And finally, we keep our spending money in the Pocket Money account, which is for daily spending on snacks, lattes, new journals, or whatever brings us little moments of joy in our day-to-day.

Systemize

The difference between a plan and a system is that a system supports the execution; it helps to actually get things done. In the Invisible System, we use technology to support our good habits and reduce the mental load of household money management.

First, if it is available, a workplace retirement plan with a payroll deduction really helps you stick with the investment account. If that is not available for you, I strongly suggest using an ACH or automatic withdrawal from your checking account to your investment accounts on each payday.

Second, use direct deposit if it's available to you. Once you have clarity on your numbers, you can use direct deposits to avoid delays in checks clearing. Some payroll companies can even split your paycheck into the appropriate accounts, although that isn't always perfect, especially if your paycheck is different each time.

Third, use prescheduled transfers to schedule your money moving to the correct accounts the same day your paycheck clears.

Fourth, use a bank that lets you see all your accounts with one log-in and with an online bill pay system to pay your bills. This keeps your bills all in one place, making it easy to set up an entire month of payments all in a few moments.

Last, use aggregating software to get a clear picture on where your money went; we discussed choosing a user friendly software earlier. The automatic data is critical for ongoing success because the idea of carving out half a day to fill in spreadsheets is not too appealing and not very likely to get done consistently.

✦ ✦
✦

Do the Work: Projecting Your Invisible System

Now that you understand how the system works, project what the Invisible System looks like for your finances. We will start with the Bills account. Take out your journal or notebook and a pen, then turn to a blank page and write "Bills" at the top. Then, make a list of all the monthly expenses that would come out of your Bills account. You can also find this activity in the companion workbook, which can be downloaded for free at https://www.cashconfidentbook.com/workbook.

Common monthly expenses include the following:
- Mortgage/Rent
- Electricity
- Internet
- Cable/Streaming Services
- Cell Phone
- Car Payment
- Car Insurance
- Private/Federal Student Loans
- Credit Card(s) Minimum Payment
- Loan Payment(s)

Take the total of your monthly expenses and add an 8 percent buffer. For example, if your monthly electric bill is $100, you want to add $8 to your monthly contribution. After a year you will be a month ahead on your bills, plus a little extra adds a buffer for changes in price.

Next, turn to a fresh page in your journal or notebook. Write "Working Capital" at the top of the page. Then, make a list of all your irregular expenses, foreseeable disasters, family obligations, and self-care expenses. Think of a twelve-month time frame for this activity. For example, if you have four quarterly payments, add the total to your page. Use a best guess for things like repairs.

Common irregular expenses include the following:
- Property Taxes
- Home Insurance
- Car Insurance
- Lawn Care/Snow Removal
- Heating Oil/Gas
- Water/Sewer
- HOA or Common Fees
- 401(k) Loans

Common foreseeable disasters include the following:
- Car Maintenance and Repairs
- New Car
- Home Maintenance and Repairs
- Veterinary Bills
- Medical Bills and Co-Pays

Common family obligations include the following:
- Weddings
- Gifts (Birthdays, Anniversaries)

- Holidays
- Family Gatherings
- Birthday, Anniversary, Retirement Parties
- Back-to-School (Books, Clothes, Supplies)
- Sports (Registration Fees, Uniforms, Equipment)
- Summer Camp

Common self-care expenses include the following:
- Clothing
- Shoes
- Facials
- Massages

When you have the total of what you will require for the next twelve months, divide that amount by the number of paychecks you have in a year and then you will have how much you need to save to stay ahead of big expenses. If this number is unreachable at the moment, just start saving an amount that you can manage and increase it when the opportunity arises. Most people do not start out being able to fully fund their Working Capital account.

Next, turn to a fresh page in your journal or notebook. Write "Important Things" at the top of the page. Then, make a list of expenses that are important to you.

Common important things include the following:

- Vacations
- Home renovations
- Anything that brings you pleasure in life that you wish to save for

Then, calculate how much you will contribute to this account each month. You do this by estimating how much it will cost. Look at how many months are between now and when you want to make this important thing happen. For example, let's say you want to go to Costa Rica. After reviewing flights, hotels, transportation, excursions, food, and souvenirs, you determine the trip will cost $3,600. Assume that today is January 1 and you want to go June 1 of next year. You have eighteen months to save. Now, divide the cost of the trip, $3,600, by the number of months you have before you go, eighteen. You want to contribute $200 a month to your Important Things account for your Costa Rica vacation.

Finally, turn to a blank page in your journal or notebook. Write "Pocket Money" at the top. Then, make a list of all the expenses that will come out of your Pocket Money account.

Common pocket money expenses include the following:
- Groceries
- Gas

- Coffee
- Lunch
- Dinner Out
- Household Necessities
- Clothes
- Shoes
- Housewares
- Babysitter
- Kids' Stuff
- Online Purchases

CHAPTER 8:

Stretching Your Financial Comfort Zone

Jenny, a brilliant young woman with a master's degree who was making $15 per hour, came to see me. She had everything she needed to make bank, but she was getting in her own way. She would find reasons not to take a better job and was considering working toward another college degree.

When we really got down to it, her relationship with money was full of hatred, fear, scarcity, and disgust. She grew up in poverty in the Deep South, and her family had a lot of resentment toward people who worked in air-conditioned offices, getting rich off them. There was a pride and sense of moral superiority with the poverty and a disgust and hate toward money and people who had it.

Even though this client went to a ton of school to be able to make a good living, and consciously she wanted to make a lot of money, her unconscious mind was not on board and was really getting in the way. We needed to work on shifting, changing, and stretching her financial comfort zone. Her "comfort zone" (it's in quotes because it was familiar but not comfortable) was struggle, not earning enough to make ends meet, and feeling under constant financial stress. This comfort zone kept her feeling a sense of connection to her family, whom she loves dearly.

I want to show you how to stretch your financial comfort zone. Why? When we start making progress, it makes changes to our lifestyles, self-confidence, how we think about things, and how we feel about things. When we start stretching outside of our comfort zone and identity, things can get wonky. This is especially true for money because money touches most areas of our life and is tied to how we see ourselves.

Money is a complex relationship because it touches on many areas of the psyche, emotions, and actions. Money shows us a reflection of our relationship with ourselves. It is also a way to group and separate people. Money impacts most of the decisions we make on some level, and the ability or inability to make those decisions impacts our feelings and ability to take actions. In this chapter, we will look at four of the major areas to look at when expanding your financial comfort zone.

1. Identity

Identity is the set of beliefs that make up who you believe you are. Your financial identity is important to understand because your brain wants you to be congruent with who you think you are. Identity can be one of the biggest hurdles people face with their finances because they just see these beliefs as true, and "the way I am" or "the way things are for me or people like me." For example, if you grew up lower middle class, you may identify as lower middle class even if you make upper middle class money. If that is the case, you will still feel money as a limit, no matter how much you make. No matter what happens on the outside, how you see yourself doesn't change unless you consciously work to change it. That's the hard part.

I had a client who was making $275,000 per year. He grew up with a single mom, and he watched her use all her money on payday because she needed to. Even though his income was plenty to invest, save, and have a good life, he was always out of money and borrowing for big things. His identity and the behaviors associated with his upbringing were still playing out in his reality.

In my experience, there are two ways that you can notice and change that identity. The sooner you do, the better you'll be able to stretch your financial comfort zone and adapt to your new financial situation.

Take Notice of Your "I Am" Statements

Start paying close attention to the words you say about yourself and how you identify in social or cultural groups. You can write the question "Who am I?" in a journal and start listing out who you believe you are, and if there are financial ideas or rules to that identity. For example, "I am an artist and artists die in poverty; their work is only valuable after they die." Or "I am from the wrong side of the tracks and money is a struggle."

"I am" statements are definite parts of your identity, and they act as instructions for how to act, think, and feel. Your subconscious hears statements that begin with "I am" as an instruction or a command, not an observation or a joke.

If you say, "I am poor," "I am bad with money," or "I am not good with saving," you're highly susceptible to becoming more of that, as you are instructing yourself to take on that identity. By saying these things, you've concluded who you are, how you act, and what you deserve regardless of reality. Your brain wants to be right, especially about who you believe you are.

You can start to stretch your financial identity by creating new "I am" statements and giving yourself new instructions on how to think and behave. Then you can start finding evidence of that statement as already true in your life, even in small ways.

Years ago, I paid $1,500 to go to dinner with a mentor of mine. We were meeting at the Mandarin Oriental hotel in NYC, which was $1,200 per night at the time. I paid $150 to park my car. I was making a lot of money, and I had the resources to be there, but I was outside of my identity. I didn't see myself as someone who went to luxury hotels, even though I could afford it. I was deeply uncomfortable because I hadn't yet stretched my identity to that level. I ordered a seltzer water and a glass of champagne for $60. I was overlooking iconic buildings in NYC, and I felt so out of place.

My inclination was to just sit and wait in the lobby because I didn't feel comfortable there, even though I had the money to be there. I literally sat in complete discomfort at the bar waiting for her. I was in a physical space that was the opposite of how I saw myself, so it was horribly uncomfortable.

From that experience, I learned that I needed to match how I saw myself with reality. Otherwise, I would be doomed to awkward bar sitting again.

Plenty of people who take home $500,000 a year feel poor and have no money in savings because of how they see themselves. Their behavior reinforces that vision, which reinforces the behavior, and so on forever.

Replace Your "I Am" Statements with New Ones

Look at the statements you say about yourself and your notions of yourself. You need to replace those with intention.

If you're making good money, say "I'm making good money," or "I'm good at making money." You're not bragging—you're just stating the truth.

As you make progress, your identity will slowly shift to match your reality.

2. Judgments

Your judgments are another way to see your identity. We think judgments are about other people, but judgment is a mental structure that separates parts of ourselves from our consciousness. Sometimes to get to where we want to go with money or anything else, we will bump up against our judgments and become resistant or uncomfortable.

Mary came to see me fully unable to enjoy her money. She felt guilty for spending money on anything that wasn't a necessity. This caused her to waste so much energy justifying her spending and basically torturing herself. We found she had a few judgments that were the root cause of her suffering. She believed it was responsible and good to save and invest, but it was wrong and irresponsible to spend on any sort of enjoyment or luxury. She was on the wrong side of her judgment for things as simple as buying her kids a treat. We balanced this judgment by seeing how not enjoying the present moment with her family wasn't serving her anymore. She still saves, but breaking that judgment allows her to save and spend responsibly.

Judgments are hard to see within yourself because they will very likely just feel true. The way to find judgments is to judge other people in your journal. The judgments you have about others are not about them or their behavior but about your mental structures. When you identify and question a judgment, you can consider whether this judgment is useful or whether it has become a hindrance.

The purpose of judgments is to keep you safe physically, socially, and emotionally. Many of our judgments are based on our past experiences and what we see as painful and avoiding that same pain in the future. As we grow and expand our identity, we need to examine our judgments to see whether we would have to be on the wrong side of our judgments to be successful.

Jenn started her own business and was struggling with sales. She would avoid her sales activities by organizing and doing busywork. We questioned her judgments about sales, and there were some doozies. She judged salespeople as greedy, deceitful, and bothersome, so it was no wonder she would avoid these tasks. Those judgments had to come down so she could feel good about offering and selling her services, otherwise her business would fail.

Money is a topic where everyone has judgments. The closer your judgments are to you, the more likely it is to impact you. As you make your judgments and notice the mental structures, start by judging the people you know and move out to people further and further removed from you. Remember, these judgments are not really about others but are about your mental structures and the mental barriers keeping you from your good in this life. Also remember you are not going to share these judgments with others, so really go ahead and be petty. It is for your own good.

Once you find a judgment, there are two things you can do to start the process of shifting or removing it. First, you can question whether the judgment is true and then find evidence of the other side of the truth. Balancing a judgment is the process of seeing the upsides and downsides of both sides of the judgment.

For example, if you judge rich people as greedy, you can start to question that. Is it true that rich people are greedy? Are rich people generous? Are poor people greedy? Are poor people generous? You can play with this kind of questioning to start breaking the mental structure down. You will very likely find that people at all income or asset levels can be greedy or generous.

Then, you can balance a judgment by seeing the upside and downside to each side of a judgment. Let's say we think being greedy is bad and being generous is good. The first thing to notice with this judgment is that the words have connotations; where generosity or giving without expectation of exchange is seen as positive, and greedy or receiving without expectation of exchange is seen as negative. That is worth noting because the words themselves are contributing to the judgment. Then we can look at what are the upsides of being generous and the downsides of being generous, and then do the same thing for greedy.

When we look closely, we can be both giving and receiving without an even exchange to balance each other. We have to have received something to be able to give it. One-sided generosity is depleting and exhausting. Balancing a judgment doesn't mean you will become a greedy person; it just means that you have more access to being able to receive.

3. Belief Structures

Your financial comfort zone involves your belief structures that construct outside reality. Judgments and beliefs are both belief structures, but I separate them for the purpose of this discussion. Judgments are about who you are and how you navigate the world safely. Beliefs are about the world and what is possible within it.

Money is a topic that comes with all sorts of beliefs. These ideas may have come from family, friends, TV, our church communities, and ourselves. Often with money, we have beliefs about what we have to do to get or have money, or what having money may cost us in other areas of our lives.

You have to work hard to make money. You can't have money and love. Money causes divorces. Money is the root of all evil. Money is hard to come by. These are common beliefs about money, and these kinds of ideas impact how we think, feel, and act.

Bee is a very successful municipal administrator. She came up in her career very quickly. She grew up poor and lived in a world where money required incredible amounts of work. As she was promoted over and over again, she was working more and more, harder and harder. We did the math and found that she was working so many additional hours that she was essentially making the same amount of money per hour as she was ten years ago.

As we grow and expand in our financial well-being, we have to update our beliefs about money and what is possible for us to be, have, and do. The best way to start noticing your beliefs is to start listening to your words and thoughts, especially about what you think is possible or not possible.

Beliefs can be tricky to change because you will generally have evidence that this belief is true. We can expand our mental landscape by becoming aware that the belief we have is true, but not the only truth. Then we can add points of evidence for other truths. Find a person in your life who works hard and makes a lot of money, a person who works hard and makes a medium amount of money, and a person who works hard and makes little money. Then find other people who don't work hard and make a lot of money, a medium amount of money, and little money. As you find evidence for more and more available truths, you can choose which truths you like better and want to create.

If we want more wealth, abundance, and ease, we have to expand our belief structures to be able to imagine and hold that new reality. We have to learn to think bigger.

4. Emotional Range

An abundant life requires emotional range because money is high sensation. Emotional range is the willingness to experience more and more intense sensations in the body. Writing this book is currently stretching my emotional range. As I am writing this book, I want it to sell thousands of copies and be a bestseller. That goal will stretch my emotional range. If the book does sell thousands of copies, I will have to receive new levels of praise and criticism. More people will follow my work, and I will be exposed to more sets of eyes on my work. Even though this is a goal that I want to achieve, I have to stretch my willingness to experience the feelings that come with that success. If I am not willing to experience criticism, for example, I won't be able to put myself all the way out there.

As we grow and expand our wealth, we will experience more intense feelings on both the positive and negative sides. A lot of times, it's our lack of emotional range that will cause procrastination, self-sabotage, getting in our own way, etc. When we have not considered what emotions we may experience in the process and achievement of certain goals, sometimes our subconscious will protect us from ourselves.

So learning to stretch your emotional range is required for building abundance. To help you feel more comfortable with your desired emotional range, it's important to sit with your emotions for a few minutes every day. Pay close attention to your body's sensations. What do you feel? Does your feeling have a color, emotion, or information you need to know? Where do you feel pressure? In your chest? How long has that feeling been there? A few days? Maybe that sensation will unlock an insight you need to expand your comfort zone.

Do the Work: Stretching Your Comfort Zone

Your financial comfort zone consists of Earnings, Expenses, Savings, and Debt. To find your comfort zone, turn to a blank page in your notebook or journal and answer the following questions. You can also find this activity in the companion workbook, which can be downloaded for free at https://www.cashconfidentbook.com/workbook.

Earnings

- How much do you currently earn in your position?
- What is the most you have ever made?
- What is the least you have ever made?
- Have you ever increased your income and then went back down? If so, what were the numbers?

Expenses

- Do you find yourself committing just as much as you earn, therefore creating a tight cash flow?
- Do you have a certain amount of free cash flow you prefer?
- Have you had the experience of making more money but being just as broke?

Savings

- Do you get nervous if your savings goes below a certain number?
- What is the most you have ever saved?
- How much can you have in savings before the flood gates open and every financial emergency imaginable happens?

Debt

- Do you frequently seem to have the same amount of debt?
- What is the largest amount of debt you have ever had?
- What is the least amount of debt you have ever had?
- Is there an amount that you seem stuck on?
- Do you pay the debt down but find it comes back within a couple of years? Explain.

Next, write down your current and ideal numbers in each of the areas (Earnings, Expenses, Savings, and Debt) of your financial comfort zone.

Finally, imagine the life you want inside your ideal comfort zone. Detail out the pleasure, the snacks, the excitement, the sex, and the accolades. Consider all the stuff you can help people with and everything you could possibly want to do if you weren't getting in your way. Write this down in your notebook or journal. Sit with it for a moment. We want to examine the subconscious brain, where your fear is holding you back. For all the things you want to do, complete the following statement: *I'd really hate and resent having [insert what you want here]. My deepest fear is . . .*

CONCLUSION AND INVITATION

Money is one of the major relationships in your life, as it impacts your work, time, living space, health, and the way you are able to show up in the relationships you have with the people you love. My hope is that you will implement what works best for you and that you will have prosperity. I encourage you to continue to care for yourself via caring for your money forever.

As you strengthen your relationship with money and start building the life you want, you will notice that money has cycles and seasons. Sometimes you will be in a place of stacking cash, saving, and feeling a lot of progress financially. Other times you will have large outflows and big expenditures and that is normal. Sometimes you will be in a season of planting ideas that will bloom into money. That is not the same season those blooms will produce fruits, and that's normal. Remembering that money ebbs and flows is important to avoid freaking yourself out and making weird decisions when money is on the outflow.

Another thing to remember is that your trust with yourself and money is critical to success. Money is a topic that many people don't discuss, and we end up with expectations that are conflicted and unrealistic. This can make you feel like you are bad at money or are doing something wrong. If you are ever feeling a lack of trust with yourself about money, make a list of all the responsibilities you regularly handle and all the good financial decisions you've made and make. This helps to keep your worries or criticisms in check and prevents them from getting out of hand.

Money is not simple black-and-white math. Money is tied up with class structure, identity, survival, and emotions, and it impacts most decisions. Additionally, lots of us grew up not talking about money and receiving little instruction or support. This is especially true when looking at money as a resource to build your life, rather than a limitation.

As you implement these ideas and grow your capacity for an abundant life, there is guidance, support, and community available to you. My business is Cash Confident, and through it, everything you need for continued progress is available to you. I have a series of courses on practical money management, money mindset, and money manifestation. There is a community of women in the Cash Confident Community doing this work together.

Here's where you can find my work:

Book:
https://www.cashconfidentbook.com

Podcast:
https://www.cashconfidentpodcast.com

Website:
https://www.cashconfident.com

YouTube:
https://www.youtube.com/@cashconfident

Facebook:
https://www.facebook.com/cashconfidentcommunity

Cash Confident offers a variety of services including do-it-yourself courses, coaching containers, business masterminds, and private coaching.

Cash Confident Community is a membership where women come to learn and practice building wealth. There is a curriculum of courses, support for money mindset, and trainings on wealth energetics. This community offers instruction, support, love, and guidance for each and every step of the financial journey.

Find Your Bleed is a short course on redirecting cash flow. You learn how to track your money, stop unwanted spending, get to the bottom of emotional spending, and redirect your money to the things you want.

The Invisible System is a no budget system for managing household finances. In this course, you will learn how to use technology to support your financial system, making it easy to stick to. You will learn to project your future needs and take on the financial habits that will have you saving money and avoiding credit card debt.

Drop the Debt is a course that will help you pay off consumer debt once and for all. You will learn how to change the root causes, habits, and mindsets that cause debt, and choose a strategy to pay it off.

Money Mindset Bootcamp is a course that teaches how to change your mind about money, allowing different ideas and more financial flow through your life.

30 Days to Get A Raise is a course that helps you see, own, and value all of the magic you bring to the table in your work. It helps you set prices and negotiate raises.

Life of Abundance is a course on manifesting money. There are practical exercises to raise your money vibes and feel abundant now.

Group Coaching Programs are offered regularly, and you can join the email list or follow Cash Confident

Community on social media to be notified when offers come available.

Limitless Wealth is a mastermind for business owners scaling beyond six figures.

ABOUT THE AUTHOR

Brie Sodano is a nationally recognized personal finance expert and the founder of Cash Confident™.

Hannah Rachael Photography

Brie teaches women how to build wealth and financial freedom. This inspires full life sovereignty and abundance. Her methods are holistic and fantastically effective because they address the root cause of common money problems.

CONNECT WITH BRIE:

Instagram | @cashconfidentcommunity
Facebook | @cashconfidentcommunity
YouTube | @cashconfident
Website | https://www.cashconfident.com

A free ebook edition is available with the purchase of this book.

To claim your free ebook edition:

1. Visit MorganJamesBOGO.com
2. Sign your name CLEARLY in the space
3. Complete the form and submit a photo of the entire copyright page
4. You or your friend can download the ebook to your preferred device

Print & Digital Together Forever.

Snap a photo

Free ebook

Read anywhere

Printed in the USA
CPSIA information can be obtained
at www.ICGtesting.com
JSHW080213081124
73177JS00005B/211